Praise for *Why Churches Need to Talk about Sexuality*

"*Why Churches Need to Talk about Sexuality* is the guidebook so many church leaders and congregations have been waiting for. Navigating the conversation about LGBTQ inclusion can be daunting, especially in the face of significant disagreement. The hard-won wisdom Mark Wingfield shares here will be invaluable for all those seeking to help their churches become more inclusive and affirming of LGBTQ Christians."

–Matthew Vines, executive director of The Reformation Project; author of *God and the Gay Christian: The Biblical Case in Support of Same-Sex Relationships*

"Mark Wingfield is a Baptist pastor with a heart for everybody. As a person of faith serving as a senior pastor, a man who happens to be married to a man, I welcome this book as it seeks to inform, engage, and encourage all readers, but most especially persons of faith who sincerely want to learn more about the LGBTQ members of their communities, in an important conversation about the church and sexuality. In this book, Wingfield inspires faith, hope, and love. And, yes, as you will soon read, the greatest of these is love!

–Neil Cazares-Thomas, senior pastor at Cathedral of Hope United Church of Christ in Dallas

"This book is the beacon of light that churches all over America need to help them address the topic of LGBTQ inclusion in faith spaces. With transparency, practicality, deep wisdom, and without bias, Wingfield gently teaches how to navigate this inevitable conversation. This long-awaited resource is one I will be recommending often."

–Amber Cantorna, national speaker; author of *Unashamed* and *Refocusing My Family*

"How we welcome and love all of God's children is the most vital issue facing the church today, and Mark Wingfield writes about it beautifully, passionately, and thoughtfully. *Why Churches Need to Talk about Sexuality* is an essential book for anyone hoping to move their church and their faith to what comes next."
—Greg Garrett, author of *My Church Is Not Dying*

"*Why Christians Need to Talk about Sexuality* is the honest and compelling story of one church's journey toward greater inclusion for LGBTQ individuals and families. Any mainline church thinking about moving through a process of discernment will be helped by reading about the work of Wilshire Baptist in Dallas, Texas. The church conversations illustrate the challenges and gifts of faithfully wrestling with sexuality, orientation, identity, and gender."
—Joretta L. Marshall, professor and director of the Carpenter Initiative in Gender, Sexuality, and Justice, Brite Divinity School

"In this book, Mark Wingfield walks us through the thorough, intense, and biblically serious process by which Wilshire Baptist made the decision whether or not to be inclusive of all who would come. A masterful storyteller, Wingfield sets the scene and provides a narrative that gets the reader as close to being there as nonmembers could be. In this book, there is real-life guidance for churches, families, or individuals struggling through these issues of the heart that have relevance to the greatest commandment: to love God and to love one another."
—Jackie Baugh Moore, director of the Baugh Foundation

"This is our story, our church's journey toward full inclusion of all LGBTQ Christians in the life of our faith community. It's a hard story, but good. Good things are often hard. But the way of Christ leads to a larger table where there is always room for more. Mark Wingfield's book is a testimony and testament to the joy that comes to a people when *whosoever will may come* really means everybody."
—George A. Mason, senior pastor, Wilshire Baptist Church in Dallas

Why Churches Need to Talk about Sexuality

Why Churches Need to Talk about Sexuality

*Lessons Learned from Hard Conversations about
Sex, Gender, Identity, and the Bible*

MARK WINGFIELD

FORTRESS PRESS
MINNEAPOLIS

WHY CHURCHES NEED TO TALK ABOUT SEXUALITY
Lessons Learned from Hard Conversations about Sex, Gender, Identity, and the Bible

Print ISBN: 978-1-5064-5857-1
eBook ISBN: 978-1-5064-5858-8

Unless otherwise noted, Scripture quotations are from New Revised Standard Version Bible, copyright © 1989 by the Division of Education of the National Council of Churches of Christ in the United States of America.

"Seven Things I'm Learning about Transgender Persons," (May 13, 2016) and "Painful Lessons from a Pastor's Viral Transgender Post" (May 31, 2016), both by Mark Wingfield are © Baptist News Global and used by permission.

"Appendix E: Genetics and Sexuality" by Gail Brookshire used by permission of the author.

"Appendix F: Adolescent Sexuality" by Rhonda Walton used by permission of the author.

Cover design: Lauren Williamson

This book is dedicated to the friends old and new from whom I have learned so much because of their willingness to talk openly about their life experiences, their love for God, and their desire to be part of the community of faith, even when the community of faith has rejected them. To the faithful gay, lesbian, bisexual, and transgender friends who have opened their lives to me, thank you.

Contents

Foreword

DAVID P. GUSHEE

This is an important book. I believe it deserves, and will gain, a wide readership. It does two things that I have not seen done in one book: it offers rich resources for "the LGBTQ conversation" in the local church, and it narrates exactly what happened when one sizable Dallas Baptist congregation undertook that conversation. Such a book could only have been written by a trained reporter who was and is also a minister in the congregation in question. Mark Wingfield, whom I have known for years, is a very talented minister-journalist, and it is great to see his gifts put to such fine use in this book.

The story of what happened at Wilshire Baptist Church holds considerable drama, and thus it would be wrong for me to ruin that drama by telling you in advance how it all turned out in Dallas. You will have to read to the end, and I am quite sure that once you get into the book you will want to do just that.

So let me instead just suggest that the book offers both very good news and very bad news. This news is not new to me, a veteran of the LGBTQ inclusion fight. But it is worth stating.

Here is one piece of very good news: It is possible to design a very careful congregational study and discernment process related to LGBTQ inclusion. Wilshire did it. I have not heard of another congregation that has done this work as carefully and well as Wilshire did. That process, including a number of important primary-source documents the church generated, is included in this book, which will move to the front of the line as a resource for congregational discernment processes.

But here is some very bad news: No matter how carefully a congregational study and discernment process is designed, it will not prevent disagreement, split votes, and substantial congregational losses. And it gets worse: the LGBTQ discernment process almost always leads a certain percentage of church members to forget pretty much everything they knew about the fruits of the Spirit (you know, love, joy, peace, patience, kindness, gentleness, humility, self-control [Gal 5:22–23]) and to descend into what can only be described as partisanship, factionalism, and by-any-means-necessary worldly politicking.

As a long-time Baptist, it would be easy for me to ascribe this to weaknesses in Baptist church life, and there are plenty. For example, you will note in this narrative that Sunday school/Bible study classes had done little to train Wilshire members in serious theological-biblical-ethical reflection when such reflection was needed. There is no word that the denomination with which Wilshire is affiliated, the Cooperative Baptist Fellowship, offered any resources for their journey, because, well, they had not and still really have not done so. And the voluntaristic nature of Baptist churches means that people can always, always, always leave if they are the slightest bit unhappy with what is happening in their current congregation, and so the escape chute is always greased and ready.

But more hierarchical, theologically oriented, and parish-based churches—such as the Roman Catholic Church—also are struggling with sexuality and other highly charged issues, and their almost polar opposite way of doing church has not spared them their own challenges. Then there is the United Methodist Church, attempting to "resolve" the LGBTQ issue through votes at their denominational conferences, one disaster following another until a split now seems imminent.

At one level, it is fair to say that every generation or so a moral issue comes along in American (Protestant) Christianity on which schism seems to be inevitable. In the 1990s it was gender, in the 1960s it was race, in the 1930s it was pacifism and perhaps the New Deal, and in the 1850s, of course, it was slavery. The list could go on.

But this time, right now, as Mark Wingfield points out, a new factor shadows all of American life: the increasingly taut polarization now symbolized in the unlikely figure of Donald J. Trump. Except in those churches where people have already sorted themselves out along red/blue, or Trump/#NeverTrump lines, the ability to live together in any form of human community across the yawning chasms of our politics is now in question. We wonder how ferocious Trump-apologist Kellyanne Conway and equally ferocious Trump critic George Conway maintain a marriage, and we have reason to wonder whether we can retain a country—or a church—where such differences of opinion persist. The tensions are frequently unbearable.

Did you notice that I gave one paragraph of good news and five of bad news? That's not quite fair to what this book offers. I think it depicts a very smart, thoughtful church trying to do Christian discipleship in a way that Jesus would like, which includes deep, probing, honest conversations in community about a very difficult issue. And the book also models honest, humble reporting—straight truth—about what worked, what didn't work, what happened, and what didn't happen.

Everyone concerned about LGBTQ inclusion and about American Christianity, and where these intersect, must read this book. Immediately.

Rev. Dr. David P. Gushee
Distinguished Professor of Christian Ethics, Mercer University
Author of *Changing Our Mind*

Introduction

There are three things you need to know about LGBTQ (Lesbian, Gay, Bisexual, Transgender, Queer) inclusion and the church. First, every church in America must have this conversation, like it or not. And choosing not to have a public conversation is itself a choice. The conversation already is happening in small groups and in the parking lot and will happen more and more. Every church urgently needs leadership to help guide this conversation.

Second, there is no way to have this conversation and keep everyone in your church happy. It is not possible because there is no middle ground on this most divisive of topics. You may think your church will be the exception, but it will not. Have the conversation anyway.

Third, there are LGBTQ Christians in your church right now, and they are silently watching to see what you are going to do. There are parents and brothers and sisters of LGBTQ persons in your church, and they also are silently watching and waiting. Whether you come down on the side of full inclusion or the side of exclusion, they want to know. Where you come down is not as important as that you decide where to come down. They need to know where they stand.

The intent of this book is not to force you and your church to follow the same path our church has taken. Instead, the intent is to help you figure out what it is you believe and practice and why. The policy of "don't ask, don't tell" that permeates most Christian churches in America no longer works. Today, people are asking, and people are telling. And most church members are ill equipped to respond.

One of the most vivid memories I have of growing up in a Southern Baptist church in Oklahoma—a memory that is etched on my brain in full-color detail forty years later—is of a particular day in fifth-grade Sunday school. The fifth-grade boys met in a small classroom, while the fifth-grade girls met in another classroom. The boys' teacher was Harold Crow, my across-the-street neighbor, a personal friend of my parents, and the husband of my piano teacher. He was a large, ruddy-faced man who sounded, when he spoke, as though he carried several marbles in his mouth.

In my mind's eye, I still see the narrow, pale-blue window in the second-floor classroom just behind the sanctuary balcony. On this particular day, that was a window every boy in the class would have gladly squeezed through, if only we could have, to escape the awkwardness of the lesson. Our topic was drawn from the Old Testament covenant between God and Abraham; specifically, it was about circumcision. You likely have not seen the air sucked out of a room as it happened that day. Our circle of boys, on the dawn of puberty, would have done just about anything to escape this lesson, yet we were trapped.

I can't tell you much of what Mr. Crow taught us that day about circumcision, other than he somehow got across to us the meaning of the word in painful detail. It was obvious that he was as uncomfortable as we were. It was, without a doubt, the Most Awkward Day Ever in Sunday school. But it was part of the regular curriculum cycle for Southern Baptist children. We were taught by the book, meaning by the quarterly literature provided from the denomination.

Oddly, I have no such memory of any lesson or sermon—and speaking as someone who was present at church every time the doors were open from birth to this day—about the sordid details of what the Old Testament says about homosexuality. Instead, there must have been hints and whispers.

Perhaps your experience has been like mine. Perhaps you have heard hints and whispers of what the Old Testament says about same-sex relations. Or perhaps you even believe you know exactly what the Bible says, yet you've never studied the texts carefully.

This whispered misunderstanding birthed out of silence cuts both ways. What drives traditionalists nuts is for progressives to say, "I just feel in my heart that inclusion is the right thing to do. We should love and accept everybody." What drives progressives nuts is for traditionalists to say, "There's nothing to discuss here. The Bible is clear and unequivocal." Progressives want traditionalists to deal honestly with the nuances of the biblical texts, and traditionalists want progressives to put forward an argument based on more than emotion. And in this frustration, conversation breaks down.

This book is about bringing that conversation into the light and making it meaningful. But one word of caution: Not everyone wants open and thoughtful conversation, because they regard such conversation to be threatening; they worry that their existing views may be challenged. When someone says, "There's nothing to discuss," what that person really means is, "I'm not open to new information that might change my mind."

Have the conversation anyway.

1. Our Story

For five years running, the most-nominated person in our congregation for ordination as a deacon was a gay man. Church leadership—including me—didn't know what to do about that. We weren't anti-gay, but we weren't pro-gay either. We were a "don't ask, don't tell" kind of church. Sure, we had gay and lesbian people among us, but no one wanted to talk about it.

In a Baptist church, the office of deacon is the highest affirmation of lay leadership and often the most-vetted role of lay leadership. And in our church, as in most Baptist congregations, the road to ordination begins with nominations from the church at large.

This man (let's call him "Adam" here) met every definition of what our church aspires to see in a deacon: selfless service, kindness, generosity, wise counsel, deep engagement in the life of the church, ministry leadership, faithful attendance, and evidence of a maturing spiritual life. The first three years Adam was nominated for deacon service, our senior pastor set aside the nomination and didn't pass it to our Deacon Nominating Committee. His rationale was that the church wasn't ready to debate whether we should ordain a gay man as a deacon. To do so would be divisive for the church and potentially embarrassing for Adam, who at this point had no idea he had been nominated so frequently.

All this, even though our church had voted in 1991 (more than twenty years earlier) to ordain women and divorced persons as deacons—a move that was radical among Baptists at the time. Those two affirmations had passed with 67 percent and 70 percent majorities, respectively, and after the passage of time, no debate remains about whether this was right or wrong; it's just who we are. Our long-tenured senior pastor intuitively knew that the question of ordaining a gay man was different.

The fourth year Adam was nominated for deacon service, our senior pastor took the nomination to the committee and said, "We need to talk about this, but I don't think the church is ready for this." The committee said, "Yes, we need to talk about this. And if he's nominated so highly again next year, we'll have to address it." Then sure enough, the same thing happened the fifth year: Adam was the most-nominated person for deacon service.

At that point, the nominating committee turned to our senior staff and deacon officers for guidance. A plan was outlined to create a blue-ribbon study group the next fall. But in the meantime, two other important things happened that summer.

The first was the ruling by the United States Supreme Court in June 2015 legalizing same-sex marriage. Not only did this raise awareness of the debate about LGBTQ inclusion in church life, it required churches to think about their wedding policies. While some—including our state denominational body—advocated writing restrictive language into their bylaws, churches like ours that were truly "don't ask, don't tell" were forced into a new era of asking and telling. And the possibility of same-sex marriage drove away one of the greatest arguments against gay and lesbian leadership in the church: that there was no means for same-sex relationships to be codified and blessed in a way that leads to monogamy.

The second thing that happened before we could name a study group was the continuation of a pattern that had been unfolding for two years. That summer marked the fifth time that a young adult who had grown up in our church came out as gay or lesbian or bisexual. In the span of two years, five of our own had gone public with their same-sex orientations. This typically happened while the person was in college or upon graduation from college. And time after time, these men and women came to one of our pastors and asked, "Will I still be welcome in the church where I grew up?" or, "I would like to come back here after college, but would I be allowed to serve or to take on any leadership role?"

Behind the scenes, all these events combined to create a spiritual unease in our senior pastor, who, although well known as an advocate of progressive theology among Baptists, had read the Bible as prohibiting same-sex relationships. On this issue, he remained the most cautious member of our pastoral staff. But the present realities before him—the number of friends and church members who were expressing same-sex orientation along with deep Christian faith—caused him to dig deep spiritually. And he found himself coming out on the other side of the question, what he would describe as a 180-degree turn that had been slowly developing over decades.

Yet he knew that his own change of view might be ahead of the thinking of the congregation at large. Even though there was an increasing drumbeat from younger members in particular (but also from some senior adults) to open the church to full inclusion for LGBTQ members, there were other voices expressing unwillingness to consider the question. He felt an intense pressure to keep the church afloat, to avoid schism, to keep staff employed, and to avoid being distracted from the big picture of the church's mission.

The stakes were high: we were an affluent and well-regarded church with three thousand members and a $5 million annual budget. Was it worth risking that to have a conversation about LGBTQ inclusion?

The choice was vexing: become more open and preserve the future generation of the church or keep the status quo and preserve the builder generation of the church. Surely there was a way to thread the needle and minimize the losses.

2. Process and Transparency

If I never hear the words *process* or *transparency* again, that will be fine. As we embarked on what would become an eighteen-month study process, no other words were bandied about as criticisms more than these. From my vantage point on the inside of the process, I saw great care and caution and transparency from the beginning. Critics, particularly those who thought we shouldn't be discussing this issue at all and those who innately feared an inclusive outcome before a word had been spoken, immediately and repeatedly questioned the process and saw a lack of transparency. After reading the following paragraphs about our process and transparency, you may judge for yourself whether these critiques were justified.

After our process had run its course, I learned from Matthew Vines, author of *God and the Gay Christian*, that nearly every church he knows of that has moved through a process that resulted in full inclusion was critiqued from the inside about process. This one word, it appears, is the most common complaint within churches addressing the question of LGBTQ inclusion.

From my perspective, our process was meticulous, transparent, and lengthier than that of any other church I've known. But from the perspective of our critics, our process was a setup to codify a foregone conclusion.

Several months after the vote for full inclusion, a longtime friend who was leaving the church over our decision met me for lunch. After enduring a full hour of criticism, I asked this friend, "What process could you envision that we might have undertaken that would have been acceptable to you and also would have allowed the possibility of the decision we came to?" The answer was that a "proper" process never would have led to this outcome of full inclusion.

Not every critic was so bold to say that out loud, but that was the frequent implication: if the process had been done "properly," a different decision would have resulted. For some, that meant a process that would have resulted in a stalemate or maintaining the status quo. There were few people in our congregation who wanted to be more restrictive than we already were; more often, they wanted to keep "don't ask, don't tell" alive. For a few, the right process would have allowed them to stack a committee to their liking.

In my twenty-one years as a denominational journalist and newspaper editor before becoming a pastor, I learned that often (but not always) people assume you have acted in the way they would have acted if they had been in your position. Often, readers would call to lodge a critique of a story or editorial and begin by saying, "I know you'll never print my opinion, but . . ." In reality, those were the opinions we most wanted to print out of fairness, but the critics seldom understood that. If they were the editor, they would not print opposing opinions. Thus, I understood that for some to assume our study group was "stacked" from the outset sometimes said more about the critic than the process.

I'm sure critics of our process would give a different account of these things than I have given. What I'm reporting here is my perspective from inside the process. And therein lies part of the rub: not everyone can be inside the process. That is a stumbling block from the outset.

The most ironic demonstration of this occurred several months into the weekly meetings of our Inclusion and Diversity Study Group. In a spirit of transparency, I had been listing the weekly meetings in our published church calendar, so the congregation would know we were working. One Sunday afternoon, about an hour into the meeting, a kind and gentle member of the congregation popped in and took a seat on the edge of the room. It fell to me to quietly let this friend know that this was a closed meeting—to which she rightly replied, "Well, that's ironic for the inclusion group to have closed meetings."

She was right, yet the level of trust needed by that nineteen-member group in order to have difficult conversations required confidentiality. The work was intense, the reading was exhaustive, and the conversations were emotional. To allow spectators to these gatherings would have easily given the wrong impression of content and would have chilled open dialogue.

This necessary confidentiality only fed the suspicions of some who already believed the church was veering in the wrong direction on other issues. A member of the study group reported this from a conversation with two senior adult couples in her Sunday school class: "They have been concerned for a number of years about the direction our church is going, feel we are becoming more a social-service organization than a purveyor of the gospel, that we are more concerned about helping people than telling them about the gospel, that we are not concentrating on evangelism."

One of those longtime members previously had complained to our pastor that the church's emphasis on advocating against payday lenders in our community was a concern "straight out of the Democratic National Committee's playbook." My response was that this advocacy was straight out of the Bible, where Jesus preached against usury and taking advantage of the poor. But in the highly politicized culture of these times, defending a party affiliation often overcomes understanding religious teaching.

The point is that any church undertaking a study of LGBTQ inclusion will begin with preexisting concerns in the congregation about a variety of other issues. And they all will get tangled up in the concerns about this issue.

Six months into our study process, our long-tenured senior pastor lamented to the group, "The biggest disappointment I've experienced in the past twenty-six years has been wondering what we have done to build up the kind of mistrust we have found here. We have a lot of mistrust of the process because of anxiety about the outcome."

Our church leadership chose to use a representative group of lay leaders to study and pray and reason on behalf of the church at large. I still maintain that this was the correct choice, given our congregational governance. Other pastor-centric churches that have made LGBTQ decisions based only on the views of the senior pastor or a small group of elders have faced sharp and excruciating backlash.

It is hard to be transparent about a study in process. Many members of our study group did not know where they stood as the work began, and some didn't land on a position until more than a year into the work. It took months of listening and reading and praying to sort things out. To drop in on one week's conversation would give a sounding of that moment in time but not an accurate understanding of all that was going on in people's minds and spirits.

Our study group did give periodic reports to the deacons and to the church at large, but no amount of information we could give was enough to satisfy the eager and inquiring minds of the congregation. From the outside looking in, the process appeared either too slow or too fast. Repeatedly, we heard congregants implore us either to "slow down" or to "wrap this up soon."

How your church goes about this will depend on the culture and governance of your church. Understand that whatever process you choose, you will be criticized, and you will second-guess yourself. There is no perfect process.

Another caution is to be prepared to face abusive personalities in the congregation who have been tolerated or overlooked during more normal times. Just as families become accustomed to the abusive behavior of a parent or child or aunt or grandfather—to the point of accepting this behavior as oddly normal—so too can churches become unable to recognize the destructive behaviors of some members. Every church has within it men or women who are bullies or mean-spirited or fear factories. Having a conversation like this will bring such dysfunction to the forefront.

I can find no other proper word to describe a few of our unhappy members than *bullies*. There is a difference between someone who kindly disagrees and someone who objects to every little thing and always demands to be heard. Even within our deacon body, these dysfunctional members were tolerated, and few people wanted to confront their behavior. "That's just John being John," they would say, shrugging their shoulders and moving on.

But when the stakes are high and the debate intense, these harsh personalities stand out and become more aggressive. Someone in your system needs to be ready to call them out and demand better behavior. And it shouldn't have to be the pastor.

3. Getting Started

In our church's recent past, there were three other occasions when special study groups were named. As a layman, before becoming a pastor, I chaired one of those. Memories diverge on how those three study groups were named, and I have searched the minutes of deacons' meetings and church conferences to try to put this to rest without success.

We began the LGBTQ study process following what we believed to be the same process used the previous three times: asking the deacon officers to appoint a study group that would report back to the deacons, who in turn could choose to report to the congregation or not. A study group in 1991 examined and then recommended allowing the ordination of women and divorced persons as deacons. The other two study groups were related to opening the church's membership policies to acknowledge Christians who had been baptized in different modes or as infants. The first of those membership studies resulted in a draw. As a deacon, I chaired the second membership study group, which met for two years. As far as I can tell, and to the best of our senior pastor's memory, all three of those groups were appointed by deacon officers, so that was how we proceeded with what would be known as the Inclusion and Diversity Study Group.

A side note here about that name: We struggled with what to call the group, seeking a name that would not appear to tilt the scales one way or the other. Multiple names were rejected. The final name was drawn from our strategic-planning process, which had shortly before this identified "inclusion" and "diversity" as the two top values our congregants identified with the church. Of course, both words carry a wide range of meanings. The name also echoed what we knew to be an increasingly common interest in academic and workplace conversations.

Over time, traditionalists on the study group and in the church chafed at the very name of the group. Explained one, "We are concerned about the use of the words *inclusion* and *diversity* in our group's work, because this makes it look like those in the minority are not in favor of these words."

Critics of our process also believed the study group should have been appointed by popular vote of the deacons—or that they personally should have been in the room when the group was named. While that last point may sound outlandish, the reality is that a few longtime members believed we dishonored them and their families by not consulting them first.

No good deed goes unpunished, it seems, and that was the reaction I and other church leaders had to this criticism. We knew how painstakingly the nineteen-member group had been chosen. We knew who had turned us down. We knew the attempt to create diversity within the group. We knew the names that had been floated by some (and yet rejected) that would have been easily perceived as stacking the deck.

Over the course of a couple of months, our senior pastor and I and our deacon officers wrestled with names. We had five firm criteria:

1. We would not appoint anyone who had a publicly known opinion for or against LGBTQ inclusion.
2. We would seek diversity in ages and gender and length of time in the church.
3. We would seek to ensure that most major constituency groups within the church felt they had a voice at the table.
4. We would choose only people who had demonstrated an ability to engage in critical thinking, to study and pray, and to be open to conversation.
5. We would choose only people who were invested strongly in the church by presence, service, and giving.

The final group ranged in age from seventeen to seventy-six and included eight women and eleven men. Of the group, one was a teenager, three were single adults, and fifteen were married. Six of the group had preschool or school-age children at home. What we did not have among the group was anyone who identified within the LGBTQ community. That was a challenge because of the "don't ask, don't tell" policy of the church. We knew we had gay and lesbian members among us, but we weren't entirely sure who they were. To balance this absence, the study group on several occasions invited members of the LGBTQ community or their family members to speak to us. Even then, some critics who were keeping score at home wanted us to balance every pro-LGBTQ speaker with an anti-LGBTQ speaker.

Both our senior pastor and I were named nonvoting members of the study group to provide theological and logistical support only. Even that was controversial among the cautious and the concerned. Some feared that our personalities were so big that we would inevitably steer the study in our favored direction. Some fretted that the mere appearance of our involvement would make the study look rigged.

My argument in return was to ask why on earth the church would appoint a group to study the most difficult and controversial issue in the church's history by excluding the staff leadership of the church and removing anyone with theological training. It was essential, in my view, for the study group to be anchored in the life of the church, which is linked to staff leadership, and for there to be theologically educated voices around the table. Further, as staff leaders, we would be responsible for explaining and implementing whatever the study group recommended, which would be hard to do from the outside.

Throughout the study process, this fear persisted. On the one hand, it could have been a compliment for anyone to think George Mason or I could bend nineteen other strong-willed people to our perceived agenda. Yet on the other hand, it was insulting to know that some members of the church thought so little of staff leadership.

In part because of this concern, I became the recording secretary to the group, creating copious minutes of every meeting and seldom speaking unless asked a direct question—which happened often.

The process was aided by an incredibly competent chairman, a young adult who currently serves as the chief financial officer of a multibillion-dollar company. He previously had served as chair of our personnel committee and our finance committee and was trusted widely within the congregation. And his views on the subject at hand were scrupulously unknown.

The Inclusion and Diversity Study Group was named in September 2015 with the following mandate as published for the congregation:

> The Inclusion and Diversity Study Group is being appointed by the deacon officers to give guidance to the deacons and pastoral staff in understanding and responding to current issues of sexual orientation and their relationship to what it means for Wilshire to be an inclusive and diverse community of faith seeking to follow the way of Christ in our time. Specifically, the group is asked to study (1) what limitations, if any, should be placed on deacon service and other leadership roles in the church; (2) what limitations, if any, should be placed on ordination to the gospel ministry; (3) what limitations, if any, should be placed on marriages performed at Wilshire and/or officiated by Wilshire staff members; and (4) what limitations, if any, should be placed on family dedications performed at Wilshire. The study group is asked to report back to the deacon body as soon as feasible but to take time for all necessary study, prayer and research. Ideally, this group will report back no later than April 2016.

On the Sunday the formation of the study group was announced, the partner of the gay man who had been repeatedly nominated for deacon service stood up in his Sunday school classroom and declared that this study was not needed because the Bible is clearly against same-sex relations and there's nothing to study. Truth is indeed stranger than fiction.

A couple of weeks later, I had lunch with this friend to seek understanding of what had transpired. What I learned was that the two men were indeed partners when they came to the church, but that had ended about two years ago, even though they continued to be good friends, share a residence, and come to church together. This man told me he had experienced a period of significant spiritual renewal in the last two years, sparked by listening to radio and TV preachers such as David Jeremiah and Joyce Meyer. As a result, he had moved away from his previous identity as a gay man.

"No one ever asked us if we were still partners," he lamented. "People made assumptions about who we are." To which I replied, "That's the nature of being a 'don't ask, don't tell' church. We don't ask anyone that question."

4. The Pain of Silence

The story was shocking when it got back to me. Through a series of odd channels, one of our staff members connected the dots and realized that a painful story she had heard about an unnamed young man grappling with his sexuality was about a student who had grown up in our church from birth.

As often happens, when this young man went away to college, he found the space to admit what he had known but couldn't admit at home: He was gay. At the same time, all the tapes were playing in his head from being raised in the religiously conservative climate of North Dallas, being involved in the conservative campus ministry Young Life, and having a neighbor (who was one of our church members at the time) tell him, "If you're gay, you're going to hell." The dissonance this created caused this young man to begin physically harming himself, which also led to a series of other unanticipated outcomes that reverberate to this day.

At first, I was defensive: "He didn't hear that condemnation here at Wilshire." Which was largely true; we were not preaching or teaching against same-sex orientation. We were not that kind of church. But then I realized a damning corollary: he didn't hear any alternative message here either. We gave him no resources to counter the hate and fear he heard elsewhere. And in that failure, we were complicit in his self-harm.

This story haunted me for weeks—in part because of how well I knew this young man and his family, and in part because of the failure I felt as a pastor. How could this have happened in our loving community of faith?

Thus, this one story became a tipping point for me in the matter of LGBTQ inclusion and the church. It is because of this young man that I realized it is not enough not to condemn; it is not enough that we "don't ask, don't tell."

As mentioned in chapter 1, over the course of about two years leading up to our congregational study, five young adults who had grown up in our church from birth had come out as gay, lesbian, or bisexual. Each of their stories is as unique as they are, yet there are some common threads. Every one of them found the courage to come out after they left the care of our youth group—typically when either entering or exiting college. While that timing is typical for many in the LGBTQ community, the stories we've heard indicate that local culture played a role in timing as well.

One young man noted that he had been unable to distinguish the Christianity of Young Life from the Christianity at Wilshire. Or at least that there was a nagging fear. Even though he was born into our church, was baptized here, and was present every time the doors were open, he couldn't be sure how he would be received in his own church. And he didn't come out earlier because he saw how gay kids were treated at his high school. He just wanted to be himself; he didn't want to be one of those "gay kids," so to speak. After moving far away to college, he felt like he could just be himself in a place where being gay was a nonissue.

Some families were immediately accepting and understanding; some struggled mightily to understand that their child was not who they thought she was and would not live the kind of married-with-children life they had dreamed of as future grandparents. Few of these families came to church and talked about this news with their Sunday school classes or friends; most of the conversation happened behind the scenes. And for the church, life went on without a ripple.

When these young men and women came to visit with George Mason, our senior pastor, they usually asked him if they would be welcome to come back into the church after graduating from college. Would they be able to hold leadership positions in the church that had raised them? Would there be a place for them, now that he knew this secret about them?

A couple of these family struggles overlapped the church's study period, creating tremendous stress in families as they dealt with the same difficult issue at home and at church. One of the lessons this taught us is that each family has to tell the story in their own way and in their own timing, and each child of the church who wrestles with sexual orientation or gender identity must be in control of their own story. Neither the church nor the church's leaders should take control of that story for any purpose.

Some of the events to be described later in this book ultimately forced the hands of a few adults and families, who went public because they felt an obligation to speak up. In one case, the grown child of a longtime member found the courage to confront their father who was opposed to the church's move toward inclusion. For two decades, this child had not come out to their parents. Then this burst forth: "Don't you see that when you oppose gay and lesbian participation in the church, you're opposing me?"

As divisions grew in the final stages of the study and vote, some of the young adults away at college wrote to the deacons or the church at large to tell their stories. One wrote, "When I felt like I couldn't tell anyone that I was gay, I turned to fellow youth group members for comfort and security. My Sunday school teacher was the first adult I ever came out to and offered me wisdom and guidance like no one else could. These people were people I knew I could trust and would love me unconditionally because I grew up being taught that Wilshire would always show me the deepest and most unreserved support. I'm disheartened by the fact that a recent divide in the church could put those who are in the same shoes I was in in a position where Wilshire may not be the safe space it was to me."

Another wrote, "As I've grown up at Wilshire, many of you have been instrumental presences in my life. You've given me Bible verses to memorize in Sunday school when I could barely read; you've been frustrated with me at VBS when my elementary-school energy was (somewhat) hard to rein in; you've cried with me when my family members have passed away; you've cheered me on when I tried teaching music to children in the Dominican Republic; . . . you've given me graduation presents."

Coming out as gay "was very difficult for me to do because, as someone who generally avoids making waves, the last thing I wanted to do was upturn the expectations my parents had developed for me since my birth. I didn't want to potentially deal with my friendships altering in any way. I wanted to maintain the status quo. At the time, I did not anticipate the shift Wilshire was about to undergo. And I certainly have *never* wanted a rift to divide my Wilshire family."

He continued, "I love my God. Because of the message *you* instilled in me as I grew up, I know that God did not make a mistake when he made me. You raised me to believe that committing a sin implies having made a choice. I did not make a choice to be gay. Being gay was not a fad I latched onto when I moved to [college]. I *did*, however, make a choice to embrace myself, and that, in turn, meant being honest with the people in my life. That is a choice I do not and will never regret or apologize for making.

"You've taught me what it means to follow Jesus's example. How to demonstrate compassion, forgiveness, and unconditional love for all people. You've shown me that love is always better than hate. But for you to then fight for a continuation of a system at Wilshire that is exclusive—a system that limits opportunities for members of the Wilshire family who are simply living to the fullest extent the lives that God designed for them—is a double standard. And one that causes a lot of pain."

5. Where We've Come From

None of us enter this conversation with a blank slate. We all have stories from the past, regrets, family members, and friends to deal with. We all have a history that, if we are open, should inform our future. Four bits of history weighed heavily on Wilshire's psyche as we entered this conversation about LGBTQ inclusion.

The first is that our long-tenured senior pastor had been on a journey himself about understanding human sexuality and same-sex attraction. In the not-so-distant past, two gay staff members had left our employ, one specifically because he decided he could not live in the closet anymore.

The second is that in the 1980s, our church had made a fear-based decision in the midst of the AIDS crisis. A young mother contracted HIV through a tainted blood transfusion. She, in turn, passed the virus to her two children. Armed only with the little information known at the time and experiencing a sense of fear, our church declined to allow the older child to attend Sunday school. In hindsight, that was a painful example of allowing our own ignorance to cause us to act out of fear more than love.

The third is that in 2008, we lost a small group of families because our staff would not promise to teach always that same-sex attraction is wrong and sinful. Our annual youth choir mission tour had gone to Boston that summer, arriving on the weekend of the Pride Parade. When our youth sang in a historic Boston church that Sunday morning, the pastor talked about the parade. Back home, some parents (including those with no children in the youth group) researched the churches where our choir sang and determined the staff was trying to indoctrinate our youth to accept same-sex relationships.

Rumors flew, and protective parents jumped to alert. Over the course of several meetings and many conversations, our senior pastor and youth minister were pushed to declare that they would always teach the inherent sinfulness of same-sex relationships. Both declined to do so.

Some parents accused the staff of seeking to "turn kids gay" and determined they could not be part of such a congregation. We lost six to eight families over this. And when they left, we thought the criticism had gone, too. However, once the study group was named seven years later, the slumbering critics of that previous episode were brought to life. For some, there was a clear connect-the-dots path from the 2008 choir tour to the recommendation of the study group.

The fourth influential part of Wilshire's background is that just one year before the study group was named, we had gained international notoriety as "the Ebola church." Thomas Eric Duncan traveled from Liberia to Dallas in the fall of 2014 to see his fiancée, a woman named Louise Troh. They'd had a son together nearly two decades before, but the randomness of United States immigration policies had kept them apart for that time.

Just a few months before Duncan's trip to Dallas, Louise had joined our church. So when he inadvertently carried Ebola from Liberia to the United States, our church member's small apartment became ground zero. And when Louise and three of her family members had to be quarantined in an undisclosed location for a month, our senior pastor and I became her media spokespersons to the world. The first Sunday morning of this crisis, I looked up into our balcony and saw fifteen TV news cameras lining the rail. In the vacuum of information available and in the midst of panic across Dallas, we had the opportunity to preach a message of faith over fear. The notoriety of that unique witness instantly became part of our institutional identity and memory.

Aside from all these influences, individual members of the congregation had their own experiences, biases, and perspectives. Most of these were unspoken, and many of these ideas were so deeply buried inside individuals that they were not able to articulate why they believed the way they did.

To try to get a better understanding of where we were starting, we used a simple four-question survey with our deacons and then with the study group when formed. The survey asked individuals to describe where they thought we currently were and where they thought we should be. These were the four options:

1. We condemn gay relationships as sinful and exclude gay people from our church.
2. We tolerate Christians who are gay among us under an unwritten "don't ask, don't tell" policy.
3. We welcome gay people as members but do not ordain or marry them.
4. We offer to our members who are gay the same rights, privileges, and blessings we offer to all our members.

Only one deacon and no one in the study group saw us falling in category one. And only two deacons and no one in the study group saw us falling in category four. The overwhelming majority of both groups saw us falling in the middle two categories, with greater numbers choosing category three. This accurately captured our "don't ask, don't tell" policy and the unspoken barrier on same-sex marriage and ordination. However, when asked where they thought the church *should* be on these same four options, the majority of deacons (69 percent) and study group members (73 percent) said category four, offering to our members who are gay "the same rights, privileges, and blessings we offer to all our members."

Eighteen months later, that was exactly where we came down in the final recommendation from the study group and the deacons. And that was close to the same percentage split on the congregational vote that followed.

However optimistic that majority opinion looked at the outset—perhaps aided by the optimistic belief that more people might change their views—it became more sobering when the minority of opposing views became feet walking out the door of the church.

Our church had a history of holding together through previous challenges. We did not see ourselves as a congregation that was prone to split or even splinter. We had lost quite a few members after the 1991 vote to ordain women, but that was more of a steady trickle than a mass departure. We had survived the Ebola crisis, and the entire congregation was proud to have been a light in the darkness of those days. To many, navigating Ebola offered redemption for the missteps of the AIDS crisis. We weren't going to make those kinds of mistakes again.

Stability could have been our middle name. We often described ourselves as a "healthy traditional church." Our membership and attendance had held relatively steady for decades, like a river seeking its level in the ebbs and flows of life.

Keep in mind that when our study process began, our senior pastor, George Mason, had been at Wilshire for twenty-six years. Just the year before, we had joyously celebrated his twenty-fifth anniversary—a milestone seldom seen in churches today, yet one that we understood to be our destiny. His predecessor, Bruce McIver, had served the church thirty years. Part of the way we understood our history was wrapped up in the word *stability*.

Thus, when a long-tenured member of the study group repeatedly declared, "Whatever way this turns out, this is my church, and I'm not going anywhere," we had reason to believe that was true. And when it turned out not to be true, we were stunned.

Our identity with stability and with adaptation were coming into conflict. Yet we thought we could navigate these troubled waters. Often, I explained to friends, "If any church can work through this, it is Wilshire."

At the first meeting of our study group, George gave this charge to the group based on his own journey:

> For a long time, I have dealt with what my view of this is going to be. There came a point at which I knew in my heart I had to make a change and be clear about it. Whether you will agree or disagree is up to the work of the Spirit. I love our church, and I don't want to bring anything into it that will hurt it. I also don't want to be responsible for being the one

who takes us down a path that will be harmful to the church. But I'm not afraid anymore.

Whatever you decide, if it means ultimately that I am not your pastor, I am OK. I don't think that's what it's going to mean. But I can't be duplicitous about this anymore. Somehow you have to help me. You don't have to please me or do my bidding in this process. But do know that I feel both a burden about this and a relief about it.

Somehow, we'll find a way through this. Our church needs to be identified by its spirituality more than its sexuality.

6. Looking for Resources

One of the things that immediately became evident when the study group gathered for the first time was the lack of knowledge most of us had. Some had medical or scientific knowledge because of their professional work. Some had personal knowledge because of their families and friends. But few had any theological knowledge on the subject.

At our second meeting, a member of the study group summarized this well in reporting on a comment received from an older member of the congregation: "People feel like whatever they learned about their faith they learned from their grandparents, and now they feel like everything they were taught is being made not true." Another member reported hearing from peers that they were glad our group would be studying the Bible, because any acceptable answer to this dilemma would have to be rooted in Scripture.

The issue of education—of studying and reflecting and learn-ing—not only was the beginning point for our work but also was a constant source of agitation. To *study* something implies that there might be something new to learn. And that in itself is threatening.

Thus, our first task was to create a reading list for the study group. We needed to educate ourselves. An initial bibliography was drafted by our senior pastor, who had read on this subject more extensively than any of the rest of us. He sought to create a list that provided balanced viewpoints while avoiding fringe extremes on either side. For example, we agreed as a group that advocates of the now-discredited conversion therapy would not be included on the reading list. Members of the study group made additional recommendations, and a final list was created with thirty-eight titles—mostly books but also a few journal articles.

Copies of all the books were made available to the study group for checkout, and the group divided the list among themselves to read and bring book reports to subsequent meetings. For weeks, we heard summaries of the various books, sometimes from one member and sometimes from three or four. Copies of the books later were placed in the church library, and the full bibliography was released to the church to read along with the study group. The bibliography was divided into six topical areas:

- The Bible and decision-making in the church; personal testimonies of gay Christians
- Loving all people while engaging difficult conversations
- Loving all people while maintaining that same-sex relationships are not part of God's design for creation
- Loving all people while maintaining that same-sex relationships are part of God's design for creation;
- Understanding and loving transgender persons

Although more excellent resources have been published in the three years since our bibliography was created, there was and remains a dearth of accessible writing on some of the topics. And some of the most frequently cited writings in the "welcoming but not affirming" category were severely out of date.

This is a point essential to discernment in reading about LGBTQ inclusion in the church. Particularly among theologians and pastors who wrote about this topic fifteen or twenty or thirty years ago, caution is required to ask what those authors would say today. Over the past two decades, much new scholarship and research have come to light about the genetics of sexuality and gender, and much new scholarship has come forward on interpretation of key biblical texts. We learned midway through our study that the author of one piece frequently cited as a biblical defense against same-sex relationships wished he never had written that piece. Yet it remains in circulation, even though it is out of print.

Ample resources exist from the rabid Right, including many that are nothing more than ideological screeds. Finding the line between the ideological and the theological is a daunting task, particularly when members of the congregation frequently pass along things that reinforce their own biases.

Shaping a reading list—which is the foundation of educating a congregation—is a pivotal first step that can intentionally or unintentionally steer a decision in a particular direction. I know of another church in our tradition that conducted a "study," but all the resources made available came from a particular point of view. Our intention was to create a balanced reading list and to consider a range of viewpoints.

Remember that ideologues on both sides don't usually want you to hear all points of view. Don't be surprised when something as seemingly simple as a bibliography creates pushback. We wrestled with decisions as mundane as how to label the sections of the bibliography to avoid an appearance of bias.

The point of the reading list was education—on scriptural interpretation, on social and scientific thought, and on hearing the stories of individuals who have firsthand experience with the questions under study. Each of these points is important and bears explanation.

Reading differing viewpoints on scriptural interpretation should be an essential starting place for any faith community that says it cares about the Bible. And there are, in fact, differing biblical interpretations. Beware of anyone who says there is only one way to read and understand these biblical texts.

For reasons that will be expounded in chapter 9, it is essential to acknowledge that the Christian community is divided on how to read the six "clobber passages" most frequently cited to condemn same-sex attraction and relationships. Christians of good faith see these matters differently. To remain ignorant of this fact is to avoid meaningful conversation.

"That's what I've always thought" cannot be the measuring stick by which Scripture is understood. Neither can "I just feel in my heart this is the right thing." Both traditionalists and progressives must be able to articulate the biblical viewpoint of the other. At the end of our study process, I had more respect for those in the church who said, "I have studied all the views on this, I understand them, and I do not see compelling evidence to change my position" than for those who hammered their hardened views without listening and learning.

Reading the Bible, though, is not enough by itself. There is a difference between knowing what the Bible *says* and knowing what the Bible *means*. We understand what the Bible means when we consider both the context in which it was written and the context in which the Holy Spirit leads us into all truth today.

The year before our study began, a strategic-planning subgroup led the congregation in a churchwide reading of Adam Hamilton's excellent book *Making Sense of the Bible*. Although not intended to set up the LGBTQ study, this book would prove to be helpful in teaching lay Christians some basic hermeneutical principles, such as how the Bible was written, what problems occur in translating Hebrew and Greek into English, and how to challenge "traditional" interpretations against modernity.

What Hamilton does in this book is to pull back the curtain to a lay audience, so they can see the struggle more educated clergy carry with them to the pulpit and the classroom. Too often, the "old-time religion" that was good enough for grandma is devoid of biblical scholarship. That's a tough sell to most congregations. Yet it is not possible to study some of the most contentious passages in all of Scripture without some basic tools for biblical interpretation.

Likewise, during the summer before the study group was named, while our senior pastor was on sabbatical, we had twelve weeks of guest preachers and preaching by our pastoral residents. To bring some cohesion to an otherwise disconnected summer, I had suggested creating a summer sermon series and asking each week's preacher to follow that pattern. George agreed and outlined a summer series through the book of Acts.

His intent, he later explained to the study group, was not to address the upcoming LGBTQ conversation but to look at how churches make decisions. "How churches make decisions is all over the book of Acts," he said. "The Bible is not just about finding the six or seven passages [on the topic of choice] but how to make decisions."

Keep in mind once again that this was the summer of the Supreme Court ruling legalizing same-sex marriage—something we could not have known when planning the summer preaching series. Partly because of this timing, congregants concerned about opening the church to same-sex weddings heard in every sermon from Acts an underlying pro-gay drumbeat. This perception haunted the entirety of the study group's work.

Is it possible that our Sunday worshipers had their ears so tuned in to the same-sex marriage issue that summer that they heard more than the preachers intended? Is it possible that every preacher that summer carried a subliminal desire to address the issue? Is it possible that the Holy Spirit speaks through the preaching of Scripture in ways that are always relevant and timely?

For certain, it is impossible to separate the study and hearing of Scripture from the moment in which we live. And that leads to the second goal of the reading list: understanding social and scientific thought.

Remember that Galileo was convicted of heresy less than four hundred years ago for teaching that the earth rotates around the sun and is not the center of the universe. His scientific work appeared to contradict a "traditional" reading of Scripture. Over time, even the most conservative biblical scholars have found ways to read Scripture in light of the settled fact that the sun is the center of the solar system.

This is not to say that the Bible always must be reinterpreted to accommodate the latest scientific inquiry. Rather, it is to say that the Bible does not hold itself out to be a book of science; it is the faith story of God's work with humanity. It is narrative more than textbook, love story more than technical manual.

One of the essential tasks of having a conversation about LGBTQ inclusion in the church is reconciling scientific and medical knowledge with received interpretations of biblical texts. Too often, religionists simply discount or discredit scientific information when it conflicts with their views. A thoughtful faith seeks instead to reconcile the two or to live within the tension created between the two. Doing that requires humility.

As science and medicine and social history increasingly confirm that same-sex attraction is not a choice, Christians who affirm God as creator of all life must honestly wrestle with the question of why God creates some humans who are attracted to others of their gender. Unless you hold a hard-core belief in predestination, this will be a challenging debate. Reading, or at least being aware of, the latest literature on the genetics of same-sex attraction and gender dysphoria must accompany the reading of Scripture.

The third goal of our reading list was to hear the stories of those who are living the experience we sought to understand. This was especially important to our study group since we h ad no self-identified member of the LGBTQ community among our nineteen members. The church cannot purport to "study" people from whom we are not willing to hear. Imagine how outrageous it would be to conduct a study on wealth without talking to anyone who is wealthy or to engage a study on homelessness without talking to anyone who is homeless.

The danger in hearing from people with different experiences is the risk of being changed. It is much harder to vote against a person than an idea. Some of us are quite content to keep our viewpoints in check by surrounding ourselves only with people like us. Or as one member of our study group said, "An abomination is easy to look at on a piece of paper. An abomination is not easy to look at in the eye."

In addition to our reading, the study group chose to invite several gay, lesbian, or bisexual congregants to tell us their stories. We also heard from a parent of a gay man in the church. We did not invite any scholars or "experts" to address the group from an academic perspective. And even though our work was done in confidentiality, critics of the study process wanted to know who was speaking to the group and to keep score of how many "pro" and how many "con" speakers we heard. They demanded we have a balance of the two.

Here's the problem with that demand: it is hard to find people who will testify against themselves. We did not have any volunteers of gay, lesbian, or bisexual persons who would come tell us how sinful they were and how we should exclude them from the church. Further, the weight of historical understanding of sexuality within the Christian church falls so heavily on the "con" side that hearing from even a few on the "pro" side is necessary to even the score up front.

We did hear from one person (not a member of the church) who told us she identified as a lesbian for a period of time but now was happily married to her husband and thinks her previous life was a mistake. Even that proved unsatisfactory, however, as it became evident to everyone in our group that there had been so much more going on in this person's life than wrestling with sexual orientation.

The common thread in all these forms of input—books, theology, science, first-person testimony—is just that: *input*. Which points again to why it is essential for churches to have this conversation. A conversation cannot happen without input. Without this kind of input, this kind of conversation, we wallow in our own ignorance and prejudices.

7. "Dear God, I Think I Might Be Bi"

One of the kindest and brightest young women to grow up in our church now identifies as bisexual. I call her "kind" not only because of the way I saw her over and over again welcome other youth into our church, but also because of the way I saw her interact with my own children, who are a few years younger. And "bright" is a label anyone who knows her would readily apply. "Brilliant" would not be a stretch.

Because of the sensitive work she's now doing in far-flung places of the world, she asked me not to identify her by name here, although she is willing for her story to be told. So let's call her "Eve."

Why does it matter that she is kind and bright? I tell you that, in part, to let you know she is not an emotionally fragile, attention-seeking personality. She does not come from a troubled home, she is not lacking in education, and she is not easily confused. This is a young woman who is deeply grounded in faith, who is a child of the church, who read theology books in high school, and who exemplifies everything we might label as "Christ-like."

At the same time, she also exemplifies one of the most misunderstood and ridiculed labels placed on members of the LGBTQ community: bisexual.

Eve's acceptance of this identity in terms of the church reaches back to her seventh-grade year, when she was excited to enter the youth group. That year's fall youth retreat was the "sex ed retreat" that was offered every six years, so that every youth would have at least one conversation about faith and sexuality. In those days and for many years, our student minister was circumspect in what he could say about same-sex attraction. Even in a theologically progressive church, there were limits to what parents would allow. (A few years after this, as described in chapter 5, we lost six to eight families from the church because of concerns that the youth choir on tour in Boston had sung in some churches that were affirming of LGBTQ members.)

Eve looked forward to this retreat, because in her home—as in most—it would have been difficult to have such conversations about sex. But this retreat "was the first time I remember anything homophobic about Wilshire," she said. "It was not condemning but super-heteronormative."

Herein lies the problem with churches like ours that make it taboo for youth leaders to engage in honest conversations about human sexuality. Even saying nothing is saying something.

Eve explained how this affected her: "The larger message is that in my family, with popular culture, I had absorbed that there was something wrong or abnormal about being LGBTQ, and I don't remember a strong message from my church at that time to counter that."

The next summer, on youth choir mission tour, was when Eve admitted to herself for the first time that she feared she was attracted to both males and females. She later recounted, "I have a journal entry from eighth-grade choir tour where I wrote down, 'Dear God, I think I might be bi.' I wrote it down and didn't think about it for four years."

In high school, a friend of Eve's came out to her family as a lesbian. She was expelled from her home, a sad but all-too-frequent occurrence in the Bible Belt. This friend assumed Eve would be judgmental of her because Eve was "the most religious person she knew." Eve recalled that moment with clarity: "She was sitting in my car crying and shaking. There was a split second where I almost came out to her too. But then no. This is so scary." In that moment, Eve said, "I learned what it means to stand with LGBTQ friends." Seeing her friends' normalized reactions to this friend was helpful. "I saw there were allies at school."

Later, when Eve began to earnestly question her own sexuality, this experience became more important. By high school graduation, she had told only two people what she was coming to understand about herself. "I definitely didn't talk about it again until after my senior year of high school. One of the things that triggered it again was a mentor from debate. From him, I understood that bi was an option. That resonated with what I had been thinking."

She entered college "with a burning desire to rationalize my faith," she said. "I had started reading a bunch of theology. I wanted to find intellectually smart people who were Christians to talk to." She quickly joined the evangelical Christian fellowship on campus, a group that became "a huge pillar in my social scene."

Within this world of Ivy League evangelicalism, she still struggled to know if she could keep her Christian faith and acknowledge her sexuality. She realized there was no one in that group who would be OK if she came out. "I felt like my two worlds were divided. I went through a process of trying to be authentic with my faith and be authentic with who I am. I asked questions of myself, then asked what it would look like to be a faithful person who wasn't straight."

And then one day, clarity came. "The tipping point wasn't me personally," she said. "It was me getting upset about what I perceived to be justice issues. Near the end of freshman year, a woman who identified as bi or queer, who was in our Christian social-justice group, sat on a bench with me, and at one point she pulled up the sleeve of her sweatshirt and showed me the cigarette burns on her arm. She felt so isolated. She was putting out cigarettes on her arm. It made me so upset that the community which was supposed to care, that was actually doing things to address justice, wasn't helping her."

Ironically, it also was through the Christian fellowship that Eve met her first girlfriend. "We decided we didn't know what it looked like, but we wanted to date. I still remember praying with her before our first kiss. I was so worried about repercussions back home. Our relationship on campus was hidden. I felt like I had to leave part of myself."

Even on a campus known for its liberal views, they did not feel safe. "There's a silencing that happens when you don't know if people are safe to talk to," she explained. "There also are safety concerns, such as experiencing fear walking down the street holding hands with a girlfriend."

Many of the Christian groups on campus were not safe spaces for her because they talked about LGBT people as "others." Eventually, she found a church that was welcoming. Attending there on Easter Sunday, she heard a sermon she had never imagined hearing. The pastor said, "What if churches were places people could come and hold out their hands and show that their scars are real?" That day, Eve saw examples of other couples in a way she had never seen before.

Back home, the fears remained. There was the matter of telling her family and telling leaders of the church that had nurtured and shaped her. It took her until the middle of her junior year of college to summon the courage to talk to her parents. "I had planned for a long time how to tell my parents. I was so worried about this conversation." With her younger sister's help, she had lined up a safe place to go immediately afterward if her parents reacted harshly. She remembered her high school friend being kicked out of her house.

"We were sitting at the table, eating raspberries," Eve recalled. "And I said to my dad, 'I think you need to know that I identify as bisexual.'"

His response shocked and amazed her: "I love you, and I don't understand."

For Eve, "the order of that has always mattered to me. His first response was 'I love you.' What my dad said is, 'I love you.'"

"At the beginning I think he was worried he had done something wrong as a parent. He tried so hard to be a good dad, and somehow he had failed. But he didn't just stop there. He kept trying to understand. He sought to understand. He went to LGBTQ groups, got to know people, asked me to tell my story. That posture of seeking understanding was important." For him, as for many other Wilshire parents, his seeking became a journey that moved from fear to faith—over a period of years and sometimes with an unwanted push.

Back at the church that had nurtured her, a church that still lived within a "don't ask, don't tell" climate, Eve found acceptance from her friend and mentor, the church's student minister. "When I talked to Darren, I found support," she said. "One of the things I really appreciate about how Darren led the youth group is very much having us consider our opinions and find a theology that made sense for us. This was a life-giving way. If I had grown up in a youth group where it was really dogmatic, I don't think I would still be a person of faith today. I would not have known how to figure out a theology. Because he had taught us how to live out social justice and to think deeply about theology, I could still be a person of faith."

Today, Eve sees her sexuality as a spiritual gift. "I can talk about the relationships with my family, being able to have a more authentic relationship. And I can be more authentic in my relationship with God. I had been a person who wanted to check all the boxes. Now I had to figure out what faith meant to me. I had to trust that God was bigger than the checkboxes I had created."

That's part of how she explains what it means to be bisexual or queer. "It means you love people, that your love overflows beyond traditional boxes, that love sometimes surprises us."

Usually, people get hung up on the question of monogamy: How can you be monogamous if you are attracted to both men and women? Her response: "I don't feel the need to date both men and women at the same time. We as people are probably attracted to more than one person. Maybe my friend likes men who are tall, dark, and handsome, and she's dating someone who is short and white. That doesn't mean she needs to have another boyfriend on the side."

For Eve, it is important to have a "queer sexual ethic," and that relates back to the seventh-grade sex retreat, where she first learned about fidelity and faith as part of sexuality. "I know that I can have a sexual ethic that has integrity. I had these boundaries in my mind that did not change when I started dating women."

8. Study, Dialogue, and Prayer

The "church answer" to a vexing problem like debating LGBTQ inclusion in the church is to get people together to pray about it. While I certainly do not want to give short shrift to the power of prayer, most of Christian history shows that prayer and study go well together and that both are strengthened by meaningful dialogue. If prayer alone were the answer, all we would have in the New Testament is a book of prayers. What we have instead is a book that tells about the journeys, the debates, the study, the worship, the conversations, and the prayers of the early church.

Throughout our eighteen-month process, various people advised that we just needed to pray more, or we just needed to study more, or we just needed to wait upon the Lord more, or we just needed to sit and talk with each other more. The reality is that we did all those things; the challenge was finding the right mixture in the right timing.

As the conversation developed within the study group and spilled over into the church, five things became obvious:

1. Christians who oppose same-sex relationships or same-gender marriage do not want to be considered bigots or uninformed. There is a sincere concern among those with nuanced positions that they not be perceived as hateful or uneducated. This is a sensitivity based on a desire to differentiate themselves from others who truly are more mean-spirited. The explanation usually goes like this: "I have gay friends. I have thought deeply about this issue and simply cannot accept same-sex marriage. But that is not a decision made out of hate."

2. Those who support same-sex relationships and marriage hear the "but" more than what precedes it. Regardless of how well intentioned or kind those who want limitations may be, those within the LGBTQ community and those who support full inclusion can't get past the limitations to hear the acceptance. For example, when a

Christian says, "I love and support my LGBTQ friends, *but* I cannot support same-sex marriage," the second part of the sentence drowns out the first part.

3. Some people don't want to talk about it at all. Having a discussion requires people willing to discuss. The issue of same-sex attraction has been made such a hot-button issue in the church for so long that for a portion of the churchgoing population, there's simply nothing to discuss. In some cases, people have erected barriers of their own to protect themselves against perceived sinful thought or action, and any discussion of that is automatically off-limits, like inviting an alcoholic to an open bar. Others carry a view of the Bible and their reading of it that allows no room for new information on most any topic.

4. Some don't hear their unique views expressed in the discussion. In the rush to take sides on a divisive issue, a fair number of Christians feel like they have no voice. There are more than two sides to the question. These variations range from the extremely thoughtful to the oddly unlikely.

5. It is important to discuss the actual issue and not use proxies for the issue. Because LGBTQ inclusion in the church is such a difficult topic, and because of the fears outlined above, the conversation sometimes falls to proxy debates to avoid the main difficult debate. These are diversionary tactics that must be labeled for what they are. For example, the conversation may easily get switched to what will happen to giving, missionaries, staff, traditions, or community identity if such and such happens, rather than addressing "such and such" on its own merits. Finding ways to keep the conversation focused on the main issue is more productive.

Our Approach

Our study group determined to take a multipronged approach to engage the congregation. This process unfolded over a period of time and may not have been perfect, but in hindsight I find it hard to imagine a more open and inclusive process.

Beyond publishing the initial bibliography, the study group created three primary avenues of dialogue:

- A series of congregational information sessions
- A series of congregational roundtable dialogues
- A series of small-group meetings between deacons and our senior pastor

One idea discussed but not used was to engage our adult Sunday school classes (the equivalent of small groups in other church settings) in their own studies of Scripture related to sexual orientation and activity. The idea was rejected because we did not have a common curriculum to use, because of the likely uneven presentations that would be made by various teachers, and because opinions on these issues likely were divided heavily along age-group lines that would lead to vastly different conversations from class to class. (Nevertheless, some classes had lengthy discussions about this on their own.)

Instead, we offered a two-hour information seminar that was given six times, first to our deacons and then to anyone willing to attend. Sessions were offered on Sundays, Saturdays, and weeknights over a period of weeks, allowing the greatest possible participation. One of the sessions was videotaped and posted on the church website, and transcripts of all the presentations were posted there as well.

The format and content of these sessions was debated intensely within the study group. The intent was to share with the congregation what we were learning without making any recommendations or tipping the scales one way of the other. Offering balanced and neutral information was a priority, even though we quickly learned that "balance" is in the eye of the beholder.

Part of that discussion centered on what role, if any, our senior pastor and I would play in the presentations because of a fear that our participation would be perceived as advocacy for a particular view. During debate over this question, one member of the study group said, "Is it going to be surprising for people to hear the senior pastor say the question is whether we are treating gays as second-class citizens? That's not just informational." To which George replied, "How would you like me to state it more neutrally?" After lengthy conversation, George told about a pastor friend who disagrees with him on this issue and who has declared he has decided the issue for his church. That was not his intent, George told the group. "If I only wanted to get my way, I would have found an easier way to do it. It's not about getting my way; it's about finding the way of Christ. I could be wrong."

Yet the group struggled to determine at what point the senior pastor should explicitly make known his views. The study group nearly unanimously believed this was not the time. Later, we heard from some of the staunchest critics of the process that they wished George had made clear his personal beliefs from the outset, while others thought they heard his personal views inserted into every sermon and prayer for more than a year.

Information Sessions

The final agenda for the information sessions contained the following items:

- Welcome and explanation of what is about to be presented
- The challenge of our cultural context, or "Why are we having this conversation?"

- About the Old Testament and New Testament texts (see appendix C)
- What we know about genetics and sexuality (see appendix E)
- What we know about adolescent sexual development (see appendix F)
- Introducing a way to understand diverse views within the church
- Explanation of View C (see chapter 13)
- Explanation of View B (see chapter 13)
- Closing comments

More than five hundred people attended these information sessions, well more than half our active adult membership. The most common response was gratitude—for the detail presented, for the time invested, and for the opportunity to be challenged and to learn. For a few vocal critics, these sessions only provided something new to criticize. I am convinced there is nothing we could have offered, short of an unambiguous condemnation of same-sex relations, that would have satisfied these critics.

The videos and transcripts of the information sessions are available at the Wilshire Baptist Church website, www.wilshirebc.org.

Roundtable Dialogues

Because of the length of the information sessions, we separated out the discussion component, offering overlapping dates for round-table dialogues. The structure of these dialogues was to create tables of eight persons, intentionally mixed up. When members entered the room, they drew numbers from a basket and were assigned to tables with those numbers. Family members and best friends were not allowed to sit at the same table. Our hope was that members with different views and different life experiences would truly listen to each other and be challenged. A member of the study group was positioned at each table to listen and take notes.

However, at the first of these roundtables, a group opposed to inclusion came en masse and managed to spread themselves out at nearly every table, each person armed with charts and graphs showing the numerical decline of the church. The negative data was inaccurate and unofficial, yet it was presented with authority. These critics were not well received at the diverse tables, and the remaining sessions went more smoothly.

The diverse groups at the tables created opportunities for transcendence and for pain. Sometimes, the parent of a gay or lesbian child was able to tell their family's story in a way their church friends never had heard before. Sometimes, parents of gay and lesbian children spoke with love for their children but with opposition to inclusion in the church. Sometimes, participants felt like they were being ganged up on by others at their tables.

Six questions were given for discussion:

1. What have you learned about LGBT from your study, attending an information session, and/or participating in a discussion group?
2. What questions do you have that have not been addressed or answered?
3. What do you think should be Wilshire's stance on gay or lesbian individuals in places of leadership for pastoral residents, deacons, teachers, staff?
4. What do you think should be Wilshire's stance on dedicating children of same-sex couples?
5. What do you think should be Wilshire's stance on same-sex marriages, both at Wilshire and outside the church, and what policies would you recommend?
6. Given your perception of what the Spirit of God is leading us to do, what do you see as the best way forward for Wilshire?

At the end of the session, each table was asked to report highlights of what was discussed. The purpose of this wrap-up exercise was to help each table see how their conversation mirrored or differed from that of other tables. Here is a summary of some of the common themes expressed at the roundtables:

- "The real solution is building relationships."
- "Being made in God's image means all people matter. This is bigger than a few paragraphs about sexuality."
- "Will the gay community take over Wilshire?"
- "How will this change Wilshire?"
- "The gay community will introduce promiscuity to the church."
- "Someone committed to God who meets our criteria for deacon service but is gay could set a good example as a deacon."
- "We are concerned about splitting the church, but we are more concerned about doing the right thing."
- "There is no need for a special policy."
- "This is not just an adult topic; youth are questioning why we are not already an inclusive community."
- "We have a responsibility to be compassionate to people on both sides of this issue. Compassion should drive us."
- "The church is not going to split."
- "People are going to get mad and leave, whatever we do."
- "I'm going to be tithing no matter what."
- "A vote on this will create winners and losers."
- "I'm concerned about the people we've already lost (millennials)."
- "To be exclusive does not resonate with millennials."
- "There should be a place for my generation in the church."
- "This issue is more cultural than biblical."
- "The crux of the matter is whether or not homosexuality is a sin."
- "Does this issue have to be black and white? Could there be room for a compromise?"
- "If we're going to demand accountability for people with same-sex attraction, shouldn't the same accountability be required for

those with opposite-sex attraction?"

- "If I'm going to be wrong, I'd rather fall on the side of love."
- "When the congregation says, 'We will' at a baby dedication, does that commitment stop if the child grows up to be gay?"
- "Why aren't we first tackling the issue of race, which affects more people?"

9. What the Bible Says

Nothing drives to the heart of the debate over LGBTQ inclusion in the church faster than to ask, "What does the Bible say?" And nothing creates more thoughtless, knee-jerk answers than to ask that same question.

If anyone tells you the Bible is unequivocal or emphatic in condemning same-sex relationships, they are wrong. There is more than one way to understand each of the so-called clobber passages most often used to condemn the LGBTQ community. You don't have to agree with my view to be a faithful Christian, but to be an honest Christian, you should acknowledge that Christians of goodwill disagree on this question.

When our study group presented its two-hour information seminar to the congregation, we had to address the biblical texts. I was tasked with presenting a summary of the relevant Old Testament and New Testament texts and the multiple ways of reading them—in thirty minutes, no less!

I designed a neutral presentation, allowing the congregation to understand the two or three sides to interpreting each Scripture. My paper was read and edited multiple times by the study group until we reached an agreement that it was fair. Yet, for some in the congregation, the mere acknowledgment of more than one interpretation was an indication of my bias. Others demanded an equal word count on each side in order to indicate true parity—which is to say, you'll never please everyone, even with a neutral presentation. Have the conversation anyway.

In recent years, several excellent books have been published that explore these Scriptures in depth. Among those are *Jesus, the Bible and Homosexuality*, by Jack Rogers; *God and the Gay Christian*, by Matthew Vines; *Unclobber*, by Colby Martin; and *Torn: Rescuing the Gospel from the Gays-vs.-Christians Debate*, by Justin Lee. There is no need for me to rehash here the excellent work they have done.

Instead, here is a greatly simplified summary of the conversation about the Bible and same-sex relations. See appendix C for more in-depth information.

Within the Old Testament, four passages are most frequently cited as giving direct reference to same-sex relationships. The first two are remarkably similar, although they appear in different books and happen at different times to different people. It is likely that you may have read or heard only the first of these near-parallel accounts, which is the story of Sodom. It is found in Genesis 19:1–11.

Many who have held a "traditional" interpretation of the Bible see the story of Sodom as being about homosexuality: the men of Sodom are wicked because they want to have male-on-male sex with the visiting angels. This was true of the translators of the King James Bible, who applied the word "sodomites" to certain New Testament passages, which we'll hear more about in a moment.

Other modern interpreters—including many conservative evangelicals who believe the Bible condemns same-sex relationships—read the sin of Sodom as being something other than homosexuality. They view these stories recorded in Genesis and Judges as being more about hospitality and justice than about homosexuality as a sexual orientation. The larger part of both stories, according to this view, is the need for hosts to protect their guests, which aligns with what we know of ancient Middle Eastern concepts of hospitality.

The next two Old Testament passages are found in Leviticus. This is the book that is chock-full of rules and regulations for the Hebrew people. The two passages in question are single sentences each. Leviticus 18:22 says, "You shall not lie with a male as with a woman; it is an abomination." Leviticus 20:13 says, "If a man lies with a male as with a woman, both of them have committed an abomination; they shall be put to death; their blood is upon them."

The traditional and widespread reading of these passages is that they are explicitly clear and mean exactly what they say. There is no room or need for further interpretation. And no doubt, that has been the majority view throughout Christian history—although modern Christians have not advocated the death penalty in such cases. Yet biblical scholars today are split in their interpretations, with even some conservative scholars arguing that the face-value reading is not the best reading.

Both Leviticus passages are part of the Old Testament "Holiness Code," which extends from chapters 17 through 26. This code for living was given to separate the Children of Israel from their pagan neighbors. It contains hundreds of rules.

The hardest part of interpreting the Leviticus passages is understanding the Holiness Code in a Christian context. There are many aspects of the Levitical code that even the most conservative Christians would not see as binding on them today. But there are other parts of this Levitical code that a majority of modern Christians might easily believe still to be relevant today. How are we to know the difference? That's where the conversation needs to happen.

Like me, you may have grown up carrying a "red-letter" edition of the Bible. These special Bibles show every word attributed to Jesus in red type for emphasis. That makes sense on several levels, because historic Christianity has placed a higher value on what Jesus said and taught than on what others, even the apostle Paul, wrote or taught. So, turning to the New Testament, we might first ask, "What did Jesus say about same-sex relationships?" In the strictest sense, Jesus said absolutely nothing about this. We cannot turn to a red-letter verse that either approves or disapproves of same-sex relationships in the way we might hope. Instead, the three most frequently cited New Testament passages mentioning homosexuality all are attributed to Paul.

In the traditional view of 1 Corinthians 6:9–11 and 1 Timothy 1:9–11, sex between people of the same gender falls clearly within a set of behaviors that are not indicative of those who will inherit the kingdom of God. Same-sex behavior is viewed as similar to other things that are sinful but for which repentance and forgiveness may be sought.

A different view is that all the forms of same-sex behavior that the New Testament condemns should continue to be rejected by Christians today. In this view, New Testament condemnations of same-sex behavior include pederasty (an adult male having sex with a younger boy), male prostitution, and excessive lust—not the expression of same-sex affection in a committed, monogamous relationship between social equals.

By the way, the English word *sodomites* was introduced in the King James Bible in 1611. It is found in neither the Hebrew nor the Greek editions of the text. And on a similar note, the word *homosexual* was not used in English literature until the nineteenth century. This word did not appear in an English translation of the Bible until the mid-twentieth century. Taken together, these facts lead adherents of one viewpoint to suggest that Paul actually was talking about the known ancient practices of cultic prostitution or male pederasty, prostitution, free men having sex with men who were enslaved and who did not have the choice to consent, and other exploitive practices.

Traditional biblical scholars, however, see *arsenokoitai* (translated as "homosexual" in many English-language Bibles) as Paul's allusion to the Levitical Code, meaning a clear reference to same-sex relations. Do not get hung up on the word *sodomites*, they argue, but instead understand that the intent is to describe same-sex relations by any name.

For those who desire a more progressive view, the single most challenging text to address is Romans 1:26–27. Even some scholars who dismiss every other biblical text as not relevant to the modern debate over homosexuality see this text as prohibitive. What gets contested is the larger point Paul is making in Romans. Some biblical scholars see Paul here linking sexual immorality to idolatry. By this account, the "degrading passions" listed are the result of idolatry. Some traditionalists would agree, to a point, but quickly note that from their view, same-sex behavior is itself a form of idolatry.

Again, for more on this, see appendix C.

Apart from the seven biblical passages that are most often cited as direct references to homosexuality, there are other passages that get cited as indirectly condemning same-sex relations, often in the context of marriage. At least one of these does fall in the "red-letter" portion of the New Testament, as recorded in Matthew 19:3–9, which tells the story of the Pharisees coming to test Jesus by asking, "Is it lawful for a man to divorce his wife for any cause?" To which Jesus answers by quoting from Genesis: "Have you not read that the one who made them at the beginning 'made them male and female,' and said, 'For this reason a man shall leave his father and mother and be joined to his wife, and the two shall become one flesh'?"

From a traditional point of view, Jesus's reference to the creation story and appeal to being made "male and female" is a clear statement identifying marriage as exclusively between male and female. They find this male-female duality threaded throughout the Bible and therefore indicative of the way God intended creation to function. For this viewpoint, the "one flesh" language becomes extremely important in defining Christian marriage and more.

An alternate reading sees the "one flesh" reference teaching us that their complementarity is first their likeness as human partners, as compared to the prior creation of the animals. Their complementarity may include their anatomical difference but is fundamentally about their being different persons rather than different genders.

10. Medicine, Science, and Genetics

When you engage a conversation about LGBTQ inclusion in the church, you will inevitably wrestle with how to weigh science, medicine, and genetics against your interpretation of the biblical texts. Among our study group were several members trained in medicine, and even they took different paths through the LGBTQ conversation. Some believed the biblical texts must be understood in light of modern science and medicine. Others saw the biblical texts as superseding whatever science and medicine may teach us—but without denying or discounting these newer findings.

There are three paths through this dilemma. One is to say the Bible and your interpretation of it stand alone and above any modern science, which should not be trusted. Another is to acknowledge the findings of modern genetic and sociological studies but to carefully hold these findings in tension with a chosen biblical interpretation. A third way is to see the Bible as a living text that must be interpreted according to its historical roots and in light of the guidance of the Holy Spirit, which includes taking into account the message of science and medicine as God-given knowledge.

The easiest path is the first option, to simply ignore science and medicine as irrelevant to biblical understanding, which is often the path taken by the most conservative Christians. Here's why I think that approach is wrongheaded and dangerous: Christianity has a long history of being anti-science, and in every case, the results have been damaging and futile. The witness of the church is damaged whenever Christians attempt to make the Bible a science book and enforce this viewpoint with religious zeal.

Sadly, the problem of Galileo, noted in chapter 6, remains with us. In modernity, look at the debates over evolution and climate change as examples of Christians burying their heads in the sand

and ignoring provable truths. To deny the forces of evolution is akin to swearing that the earth is the center of the universe; just because you fervently believe it doesn't make it true. The same is true of advancing scientific understanding of sexual orientation and gender identity; you don't have to like these findings, but you do need to acknowledge their reality.

Here's the point: The church will carry forth the mission of Jesus best by engaging in thoughtful conversation rather than refusing to acknowledge new information. To some today, what genetics and sociology have to say about sexual orientation is inconclusive. That view is more defensible than to say the work of genetics and sociology is irrelevant.

In my view, and in the view of a majority of our study group, the preponderance of evidence points to the fact that sexual orientation is not chosen but is a result of a complex set of biological and environmental factors. For a fuller discussion of this, see appendixes E and F, where my friends Gail Brookshire and Rhonda Walton present their perspectives as a geneticist and medical doctor.

In what other area of life would modern Christians ignore medical research? When you have an illness, you want to know the latest information on treatments. That doesn't mean you abandon belief in the power of prayer for healing. The vast majority of modern Christians believe God often brings healing through the knowledge of physicians who are enlightened by the Spirit of God through their education.

Just as I believe there is a way to reconcile the reality of evolution with the truth that God is Creator of the universe, so I believe it is possible to cherish the Bible as a sacred text while accepting modern science on genetics.

Rather than instinctively saying, "No way," the church is at its best when it seeks the Spirit of truth to fervently pray, "Show me your way."

11. What about the *T* in LGBT?

"When I awoke on Friday, May 13, I did not know a single transgender person. I did not know the parent or the brother or sister of a transgender person. But as that day unfolded, my life changed. And I stand before you today as someone who has been revolutionized because an untold number of transgender persons and their family members have reached out to me and loved me, even though more often than not, the church of Jesus Christ, which I serve as a Baptist pastor, had not loved them."

These were the opening words of a TEDx Talk I gave in Charlottesville, Virginia, in November 2016, the very week our congregation back in Texas was voting on whether to become fully inclusive of the LGBTQ community. And that was the same week as the stunning 2016 US presidential election. What a week!

How I came to be halfway across the country giving a TEDx Talk traces back to our Wilshire study group. To explain, here's what I said on the TEDx stage:

> Months into our study process, after reading and praying and hearing from guest speakers and discussing for hours on end, a few members of the group said, "We've talked a lot about the L and the G, but we haven't talked at all about the B and the T." In answer to that need, we called upon a pediatrician and a geneticist within the study group to help us. Together, they crafted a one-hour presentation that blew my mind.
>
> My friends Gail Brookshire and Rhonda Walton explained to us the difference between sexual orientation and gender identity. We learned that sexual orientation is about who you love, and gender identity is about who you are. These are distinctly different things. We learned about the growing

body of scientific research on gender appearance and gender identity and how these get formed in the womb—usually in ways that are aligned but sometimes in ways that are misaligned. We learned about how anatomy, chromosomes, and brain cells must line up like three cherries on a slot machine for most of us to experience unconflicted gender identity. We heard real-life stories of babies born with ambiguous genitalia.

And then we talked about what it means to be made in the image of God as the Bible teaches in Genesis. Dr. Walton challenged us with these words: "We must believe that even if some people got a lower dose of a chromosome, or an enzyme, or a hormonal effect, that does not mean that they got a lower dose of God's image."

Her words echoed in my head and my heart for several days. Why had I not known this information before? Why had I not understood this before? And then the Spirit moved in me in a way I could not control. The next Wednesday morning, I woke up with the sense that I needed to write down what I was learning. As a regular columnist for the national news service baptistnews.com, I had a platform. So I sat down on that Wednesday morning and in forty-five minutes, wrote a column.

I was not able to comprehend what those words would unleash.

The column went live on the baptistnews.com website two days later, Friday morning, May 13, at 5:00 a.m. eastern time. When I awoke at 6:30 a.m. central time and looked at my cell phone, I immediately understood something was happening. On this morning, my Facebook feed and my email inbox already were buzzing. As the day progressed, my wife and I both got caught up in simply watching the column spread through social media. Monitoring it on Facebook was like watching an electric meter spin on a hot summer day in Texas. Suddenly, I knew what it meant to "go viral."

Over the next two weeks, I spent every free moment responding to email messages, Facebook messages, and phone calls. My thought was that if someone took the time to write me and tell me their story, I ought to have the courtesy to respond. After two weeks, I had engaged in more than 450 personal conversations about the column. And 95 percent of those were positive, many filled with heart-wrenching stories of oppression, confusion, family estrangements, and rejection by the church. I heard from transgender persons, from their parents and siblings and coworkers.

Most moving were the messages and calls from transgender persons who said, "You said you don't know any transgender persons. I'd like to be your transgender friend."

So in addition to emails and phone calls, I began meeting face-to-face with some new friends who are transgender. We met for lunch or dinner or coffee and spent hours getting to know one another. They were shocked that a Baptist pastor would sit down to hear from them, and I was shamed to hear their stories of pain and suffering and how difficult it was sometimes just to be able to use the restroom in peace. Six months later, I'm still meeting new transgender friends and their family members, and I'm still learning.

Almost every transgender person I have talked with has told me they knew from their earliest awareness, from when they were four, five, or six years old, that they were not the gender inside that they appeared to be outside. Most didn't know what to do with this conflict and were afraid to speak it out loud. Many tried to repress it, sometimes through misguided religious strictness. Sometimes they had no words or role models to make sense of who they were. And most of the time, when they finally came to grips with the reality they had known all along, they were rejected by their churches, by their families, and certainly by their friends.

As I write this book nearly two years later, I still have weekly communication with transgender friends who are just discovering the online column or TEDx Talk or who are following up with updates on their journeys back to faith.

I can't explain this much better than I did in the two Baptist News Global columns, which may be found in appendix D.

12. Laura Beth

The first transgender person I ever met was Laura Beth Buchleiter. Soon after my column on seeking to understand transgender persons was published and went viral, my friends Rhonda and Gail invited me to lunch with Laura Beth. That day was so transformative that I can still see in my mind the table where we sat and who was sitting where.

How the four of us came to be lunching together begins with irony. Laura Beth had met another friend's daughter, Kathryn, in a divorce recovery group. After struggling for most of her forty years with understanding who she was, Laura Beth lost her marriage when she transitioned from male to female in identity. Yes, transwomen need divorce recovery groups, too.

In that group, Laura Beth met Kathryn, who had just left her husband. Kathryn introduced Laura Beth to her mother, Mary, who is an active Wilshire deacon and volunteer.

"Mary was the first parental figure I ever encountered who was totally accepting and encouraging," Laura Beth said. "That was a huge turning point for me. And the fact that they were active in a Baptist church made that more intriguing. None of those things fit together in the world I was emerging from."

The world from which Laura Beth was emerging was conservative evangelicalism. She had been educated at Moody Bible Institute, and at the time of her transition and divorce, she was a leader in a church start in the Dallas suburbs. Her life's goal was to attend Dallas Theological Seminary, a conservative school affiliated with the Bible church movement.

All that broke down when she had to face the facts about her gender dysphoria. What forced her hand was a medical issue and a psychological issue. Surgery to resolve a painful hernia unexpectedly revealed inside her body the remnants of undeveloped ovaries.

Upon reflection, this made perfect sense, because Laura Beth had known from a young age that she was not a boy on the inside.

"As a child, I identified more with what girls were experiencing than with boys. I had to fight myself to play with the boys. To say when I knew internally was probably late in puberty, when my voice wasn't changing, my stature wasn't changing like everyone said it should, and there were physical manifestations that were not coming about. There was part of me that had always hoped I would grow into masculinity. And it never happened."

There came a moment in late high school or in college when Laura Beth finally realized this burst of masculinity wasn't going to happen. At one point, she was put on high doses of testosterone, but that only increased her suicidal ideations and actions. And her body rejected the testosterone severely.

"As I went through my low point and dealt with the suicidal incidents, part of my mandate from the doctors was to live more authentically," she explained. "That meant embracing who I was in terms of my gender identity. I knew that doing that was going to have a direct impact not only on my faith but on my career path." She began to realize that her version of evangelical Christianity required her to create a mask or a smokescreen, a house of cards.

Before approaching any of those closest to her, she determined to write a paper examining the Bible and gender identity. She needed to convince herself first that if she were, in fact, a female instead of a male, she was not abandoning her Christian faith—even if she knew in her heart that her brand of Christian faith would certainly abandon her.

"I was at a place where life and faith, real life and faith, were starting to intermingle," she recalled. "I could no longer keep the boundaries between the two that kept them clean. Life was going to get messy, and that was going to make faith dirty. It turns out that authenticity is found for me in dirty faith. Faith is not clean and polished."

Through that study, she realized she suffered from "an addiction to answers," what she now diagnoses as a common condition among evangelicals. On the other side of that journey, "there's no evidence in my life demanding a verdict anymore," she said. "I am fully OK with having questions that may never have answers. Because that's where God is."

That was the point where Laura Beth met Kathryn, who introduced her to Mary, who introduced her to Gail and Rhonda, who introduced her to me.

Gail and Rhonda invited Laura Beth to their Sunday school class. She was seeking spiritual community. She knew she needed a healthy spiritual community, but she did not expect to find that inside a Baptist church in Dallas.

She landed at Wilshire in the middle of our LGBTQ study process. "While the church wasn't officially an accepting community, I felt accepted," she said. Then Rhonda and Gail shared with her my column. That a Baptist pastor would write such a thing "sealed the deal for me," she said. "Whether or not the church would be behind this, I knew there was a safe space here." She determined that her connection to the church would not be dependent on the outcome of a final vote. But she knew that her ability to engage with the church would be.

Even so, Wilshire already was becoming a spiritual home, she remembered. "There was a sense that I had a stake in it. I had something to be gained a lot by the direction of the church." She likens this to being above the eye of a hurricane, hovering in a helicopter, and then making a conscious decision to cut power and drop down into the storm. Even in the storm, she demonstrated restraint. It was not until the final all-church conference before the vote that Laura Beth made any public statement to the church.

"I have been moved to speak, not because we disagree but because we agree on so much, and ultimately we are of the same citizenship and share the same Lord," she told the church. "I joined Wilshire even before the vote to know that you would fully embrace me and others like me. I am home here. I chose Wilshire because you are willing to ask the right questions. Tough and right questions. I don't want this to be political. I live to give the grace that I desire to be given by leaning boldly into the grace I have been so freely given. Let's find ways to graciously grow together."

Regardless of how the vote turned out, being at Wilshire during this time would be formative to Laura Beth's spiritual development, she thought. But in her heart, she knew the stakes were high. "I thought, if this church can do this, then I have a future in ministry," she recalled. "It was a catalyst for me of affirmation. Coming into it, I had a sense of that. There was a piece of me in my future, my goals, my calling that needed this work. At the same time, I was deliberately sheltered from some of the more intense opposition."

Despite her low-key presence, "there were moments when I wanted to be more aggressive," she said. "I've learned that I am not an aggressive advocate. I've been labeled an activist, and that label doesn't resonate with me. 'Advocate' is much more accurate. My goal is to come alongside. When I meet a pastor, I don't make a case; I just sit and get to be the question. I don't have to argue with them. I don't have to win. The only exception is when there is a youth involved or a family is being damaged."

Her own journey of understanding gender dysphoria is chronicled in her book *Shattering Masks: Affirming Identity, Transitioning Faith*. She measures the milestones in her journey by the times she had to build masks to disguise who she was. "There were moments through early youth groups and church encounters that I was presented with a concept of what it meant to be a Christian, what it meant to be a man, so that in order to fit the mold, I had to be something I wasn't," she recalled. "I had to repress some true pieces of me. And I did it under the guise of 'the old is gone and new is come'—but without the benefit of allowing the Spirit to speak that new into me."

As a young adult, she fought these fears by doubling down on more conservative beliefs. For example, as a male, she took an adamant stand against women leaders in the church, "because that's what good evangelicals do."

"Somewhere in my heart I knew I had learned deep, beautiful truths from the teaching of women, and still I refused to let that speak into my church practice. I dove heavy into Reformed theology and structured thinking because I was taught not to trust my own thoughts and feelings."

Yet the evidence of denial was right before her in the mirror. "If I relaxed and truly let myself out, which was very rare, I had an effeminate voice. In fact, one of our pastors at a church in Nashville instructed me to work on masculine tones in my voice, so I could speak with more authority."

The freedom she knows today of being authentic has come with a heavy price, especially emotionally and spiritually. "I still deal with PTSD," she said. "Some from specific events but some from trauma over a period of time. That entire process of hiding who I was for the first forty years of my life had an impact. I will always be dealing with some emotional impact from that. But now I have a foundation from which to deal with it."

One of the reasons this is so hard to unwind is that it took so long to get wound up in the first place. Gender identity is even more foundational to a person's sense of well-being than sexual orientation. "All the psychological issues that arise because of the dysphoria cannot be addressed until the dysphoria is addressed," she explained.

As an archer, Laura Beth likens this journey to shooting at a target: "It's one thing to be sitting still on an archery range and shooting a target. It's another thing to be sitting in a tree stand, shooting at a moving target. That's more challenging but doable. Where gender identify and sexual orientation and faith all intersect is more like being in a helicopter shooting at a moving target, being on a moving platform shooting at a moving target. Until one of those things stabilizes, the odds of hitting the target become less and less."

From her vantage point, the church also is suffering from years of denial and creating masks. "This conversation around LGBTQ inclusion is part of a bigger question of this addiction to answers, the scientific approach to faith that is misplaced," she said. "The church has been arrogant, and we're paying a price for it. My hope for the conversation is not just that we find greater LGBTQ inclusion but that we find a softer heart, a heart that is more sensitive to true issues of justice."

But before that comes to pass, she has a simpler goal: "I don't want to see any more LGBTQ youth in Christian faith communities seeing no way forward except to take their own lives."

13. What about Marriage?

The final straw for both sides in our LGBTQ inclusion debate was marriage. It was because of marriage that compromise could not be found.

It's not that the progressives on the study group were campaigning to open the church to same-sex weddings, but they couldn't find a way to preach a common sexual ethic without allowing for same-sex marriage. This was a surprise to us all. If we had found a way to be open to LGBTQ inclusion in the church with the exception of same-sex marriages, we would have lost many fewer people. We would have gained many fewer people, too. Still, many of us wanted this compromise to work.

Near the end of the study process, when for the first time ever someone in the church asked me what I believed about this (rather than assuming what I believed, which was the most common action), I answered by saying this: "If I were king of the universe, which I am not, I would lead us to full acceptance except with a delay on same-sex marriages until such a time as there is greater consensus on that issue. But that's just me, my own view." I now see that as an unrealistic and ultimately unhelpful view.

In that same study group meeting, as the group was finalizing what would become a majority and minority report, one member made what he called "a last-ditch appeal" on the issue of same-sex marriage. It was his view that allowing even the possibility of a same-sex marriage at our church would drive more people away than if we allowed full LGBTQ inclusion on everything else. If we would just wait a little longer, attitudes would soften, and the losses would be fewer.

"When the Supreme Court ruled, the earth did not shake, because thirty-eight states already allowed it," he said. "I agree that this is a train that is not stopping. I get that. We are going to lose key members over this." And then he predicted that we would lose some younger adults who, over the course of their lives, had the potential to give a million dollars to the church. "If you would hit the brakes and wait, it will come," he urged. "But if we push this through, people are going to leave, people who are in their prime earning years. You're going to get it done in five years anyway."

A bit later, another member continued the thread: "I think the biggest issue is the gay marriage. I've come to change my mind on ordination of gay deacons. When you begin to talk to people about that issue, they can come around. It's not a big issue. I'm not sure about the clergy. The line in the sand is on gay marriage."

Another added, "And the baby dedications are close to that for some people."

To which the previous speaker added, "There's the rub: The baby is put in an untenable position in that way. Nobody wants to do that, yet people ask how we can do that without affirming gay marriage."

Here's the problem that snared us from compromise on marriage: A strong majority in our congregation would have had no problem with gay deacons, gay Sunday school teachers, gay members in general. As long as they were celibate. Or as long as they weren't married. Which would have automatically applied a different sexual standard for gay and lesbian Christians than for heterosexual Christians.

For example, in our deacon interview process, we don't normally ask candidates to explain their sexual habits. We don't ask single adults if they're celibate. We don't ask married adults if they've ever been unfaithful. We don't ask anyone what kind of sex they have or where or how often. We do teach that sexual relations are best fulfilled within the covenant of marriage. That is our ethical standard and expectation. But no one wants to be on the Sexual Practices Inquisition Committee.

To say to gay and lesbian Christians, "We welcome you here and want you to be fully involved—except that because of the way God has made you, we believe you should not ever have a loving or committed sexual relationship," is to have two standards. And to say that monogamous fidelity within marriage is required for a leadership position inherently excludes anyone who we're not willing to marry. That creates two classes of membership.

Like it or not, the fact that same-sex partners may legally marry in the United States changed the equation for the church's debate. When same-sex marriage was not possible, a church like ours could not operate with a common standard. Now that we could, the question was whether we would.

The ability to marry gives every person equal hope that lifelong intimacy with a partner is possible. Further, it assures gay people that they will have the same blessing not only of a wedding but also of their marriage in the church. One gift the church gives married couples is the encouragement of stability and respect that comes with their vows. The church is a friend to marriage. While other forces such as work, materialism, youth culture, and sexual temptation mitigate against marriage, the church is there to support and strengthen it. So-called partnerships or civil unions always bear a stigma that they are marriage-like but not marriage. With marriage equality, young people growing up gay in church will have the same sense of promise that they can remain in church and have a healthy marriage and family that is recognized and celebrated, not just tolerated.

This came down to the fine-point discussion of whether it would be OK for gay and lesbian couples to be married elsewhere and then come to the church, instead of being married in the church. Opinions on this varied widely, sometimes to the point of being astonishing. My favorite example is the member who said, "I have no problem with us performing same-sex marriages in the sanctuary, so long as the couple promises never to have sex."

Others seemed to believe if we opened the church to same-sex marriage, there soon would be couples copulating on the chancel steps—the biblical abomination of desolation. A common variation on this concern was for opposite-sex couples who had been married in our sanctuary or chapel to insist that allowing same-sex marriages in that sacred space would somehow invalidate or stain their own marriage ceremonies. This is a close cousin to the argument that same-sex marriage in general devalues the concept of hetero-sexual marriage.

A fair number of church members sought to parse the difference of one location over another. For example, it would be fine for one of our ministers to perform a same-sex wedding somewhere outside the church but not inside the church—or in the chapel but not the sanctuary, or in an office but not in a worship space, or out-doors at the church but not inside the building. All these were well-intentioned ways of seeking compromise, but they were based on emotion more than reason. The ultimate disagreement was not about location but about what is an acceptable practice of Christian marriage.

In debating all this within the study group, one member in par-ticular (but not in isolation) kept pushing that the "biblical" view of marriage is always between one man and one woman—a common evangelical Christian viewpoint. To this, another member of the study group pushed back to say an author on the reading list with this viewpoint did not make satisfactory arguments. "He starts out with a core value that marriage and sex are between men and women. If that's where you start, how do you ever reach any other conclusion? It influenced every single analysis he made," the chal-lenger asserted. "He states a conclusion and then interprets Scrip-ture to confirm that conclusion." The question, this member added, is not whether Scripture changes (he said it does not) but whether human understanding of Scripture may change. "We don't read Scripture the same way today as we did on women in the church. Scripture hasn't changed."

In fairness, traditionalists also believe progressives define a con-clusion and attempt to interpret Scripture to confirm their biases. It brings us to this chapter's question: What does the Bible actually say about marriage? And to what extent does it ring true today?

It would be helpful if more churches, Bible study groups, Sunday school classes, and book clubs would do some hard reading and thinking about marriage. Among the questions that ought to be dis-cussed:

- What makes a wedding a "Christian" wedding?
- What makes a marriage a "Christian" marriage?
- What portion of most weddings today could be considered sacred, and what portion could be considered party or event?
- Is marriage in the United States a legal commitment governed by the state or a religious commitment governed by the church?
- In the Protestant congregationalist tradition, everything else that is sanctioned as an official endorsement of a person or persons—for example, deacon and clergy ordinations—is voted on by the church. There is no history of these churches voting to give approval to who may be married. Should there be?
- When a pastor officiates a wedding, does she represent the church or the state or both? And does that answer change if the wedding is away from the church building?
- How should Christians reconcile the Old Testament witness of all kinds of family relationships, including polygamy?
- What is the history of marriage, and how has that changed over time?
- What are the scriptural passages that give instruction on marriage? (Start here: Genesis 1:26–31; Genesis 2:18–24; 1 Corinthians 7:1–9; Ephesians 5:21–33; Matthew 19:1–9; John 2:1–11; Hebrews 13:4.)

The single best resource I've found on understanding the history and traditions of Christian marriage is *From This Day Forward: Rethinking the Christian Wedding* (Westminster John Knox, 2016), by Kimberly Bracken Long. Among other topics, she discusses the history of marriage, including these points, paraphrased here by me:

- The Old Testament record of marriage in Jewish tradition acknowledges marriage as an entity but does not give much additional detail about what was meant, particularly in light of the frequency of men taking multiple wives.
- For the first thousand years of the New Testament era, the church had little to do with marriage. Marriages were often

done at home with little involvement by the clergy. Marriage was a domestic and legal category, not a church-sanctioned event.

- Marriage is mentioned in the New Testament in a few places, and we read about people who are identified in ways to indicate they are married couples. However, we do not know what those marriages looked like or how they were created.
- From the third century through the sixth century, Christian leaders wrote diverse opinions about marriage, including some who saw sexual relations of any kind as a sinful result of the Edenic fall.
- Augustine, writing in 401 CE, provided the first significant theological treatise on marriage. He cited three purposes only for marriage: (1) procreation; (2) "mutual fidelity" to protect each other from fornication; and (3) sacramental significance, to which he explained that just as one cannot undo baptism, a couple should not be able to undo marriage. Augustine brought marriage into the church.
- The earliest wedding liturgy in the Western church dates to sixth-century Verona.
- More detail is found in a wedding liturgy from the eighth century and Gregory the Great. Here we see for the first time an interpretation of couples in their marriage prefiguring the marriage between Christ and the church, alluded to in Revelation 21.
- Spain saw a rich wedding liturgy develop by the eleventh century, including the giving of a ring and a blessing of the bedchamber.
- In the eleventh century, church weddings became more common in England and France, introducing spoken vows, the giving of rings, and a kiss. We see here the early language of "with this ring, I thee wed."
- Still, marriages were typically arranged by parents for reasons other than love.
- Thomas Aquinas detailed a view of marriage that shaped Roman

Catholic thought for centuries, placing a priority on procreation as a reason for marriage and calling marriage a "sacramental grace."

- What we consider traditional wedding vows today first took similar form in the sixteenth century.
- Much of our modern idea of wedding liturgy is owed to the *Anglican Book of Common Prayer* and is tied up in the escapades of Henry VIII.
- Catholicism, meanwhile, moved to solidify the view that marriage is a sacrament of the church; the Council of Trent declared it one of seven sacraments. All couples were required to marry in Christian ceremonies with priests attending.
- Not until the late eighteenth century did people in Western Europe and North America begin to think of love as the primary reason for marrying.
- For most of world history, "marriage" was about alliances, real estate, labor forces, accumulating wealth, and ensuring legal heirs.
- From the Middle Ages to the eighteenth century, brides in Europe came with dowries.
- Some have identified a "golden age of marriage" in the United States from 1947 through the early 1960s. This ideal was the stuff of television shows and marketing and projected a desirable norm, especially for white Americans.
- In the second half of the twentieth century, expectations for marriage were challenged by the rise of women in the workplace, the invention of the birth control pill, the civil rights movement, interracial marriage, and increases in divorce.

To make a case for "biblical marriage" is to raise more questions than answers. To which part of the Bible will you turn for a definition? The Old Testament practices of polygamy and arranged marriages? The kind of marriage Mary and Joseph had? The teachings of Jesus, who said that in heaven people will neither marry nor be given in marriage? The teachings of Paul, who wished everyone were like him and single? As Diana Garland has noted, there are more dysfunctional families in the Bible than we'd like to admit.[1]

Advocates of "traditional" marriage often cite Genesis 1:27 as the end-all defense from creation: "So God created humankind in his image, in the image of God he created them; male and female he created them." If God created male and female, and if male meets female is the way the world gets populated, then that must be God's plan for marriage. By the way, if you see Adam and Eve as real, individual persons, who officiated their wedding ceremony? Or was it OK for them to cohabit before they knew better? This is the slippery slope of talking definitively about "biblical marriage." Is the Genesis story about companionship, about procreation, or about complementary body parts?

One senior adult woman who left our church over this issue told me that in her way of understanding creation, the question of what's right and wrong sexually is all about the parts: the man parts fit into the woman parts, and that's all we need to know. God made tab A to insert into slot B. End of story.

As noted in my summary list, we have Aquinas to thank for the still-prevalent notion that marriage is about procreation above all else. Even though this is not the theology of any Protestant body in America today, it has seeped into our collective consciousness in unhealthy ways. Imagine our surprise when during the heat of debate within our Baptist church, a disgruntled member distributed to his entire Sunday school class the writing of a Catholic apologist who begins his discussion of marriage by asserting that marriage is primarily for procreation.

Even Christians who don't buy Aquinas's position still are prone to elevate marriage to "the ultimate holiness," said our senior pastor, George Mason, in comments to our study group. He explained, "Paul says he wishes all people were single as he. We acknowledge, and he acknowledged, that cannot be for everyone. But in America, we

---

1. David Garland and Diana Garland, *Flawed Families of the Bible* (Ada, MI: Baker, 2007).

now believe marriage and having children is the ultimate thing. This whole matter is not about whether someone can or should get married. There are a lot of single, straight people in our church who should not feel like second-class citizens. I would like us to acknowledge that singleness is not a defective status. Second, a recognition that celibacy for some is a spiritual discipline and for some is a stage of life before marriage. The same should be true for those who are gay. If someone chooses celibacy and singleness, can't we celebrate that? Are people less because they don't marry?"

Too often, Christians who don't want marriage equality do not own up to the fact that what they really want is gay Christians who remain sexually abstinent their whole lives long, whether they have the gift of celibacy or not. They compare the gay experience to those straight persons who never marry. They are all expected to remain sexually abstinent forever.

A side note: Although the word *celibacy* has become somewhat commonly used to mean sexual abstinence, its root is actually "unmarried." Celibacy is singleness, not sexual abstinence. Similarly, the word *chastity* is often used to mean sexual abstinence, when in fact it means purity. Chastity does not mean virginity either. It means appropriate sexual behavior.

The evangelical church has muddied these definitions in other ways, especially with incessant talk about "purity." This trend was elevated in the late twentieth century by the Southern Baptist "True Love Waits" movement, which was aimed at teaching abstinence until marriage but perhaps also inadvertently taught girls that they were the property of their fathers, who were to keep them "pure" until their God-given husbands took possession of them.

A woman in our study group recoiled at another female member's insistence on the purity language of the Bible: "Talking about purity seems to be really degrading, lustful, and negative to the community. I have a hard time differentiating between a homosexual couple who has those issues and a heterosexual couple with those issues. I don't feel like this is specific to a homosexual relationship."

It is hard for straight, white Christians in America to read the Bible through any lens other than that of straight, white Christians. Who we are, our life experiences, inform our reading of Holy Scripture. Which is why all of us need to be challenged to hear the viewpoints and interpretations of Christians. Recently, I was reading a prominent female New Testament scholar who made the case that the gospel writer Luke seldom portrayed women as having agency in the stories. As a man, I never had thought of that; it just didn't occur to me to read Luke through the eyes of a woman. To do so did not change the words of Scripture but instead changed my hearing of Scripture.

This is the same conversation we need to have in the church about marriage. We need to dig down and discuss which biblical passages are about relationship and which are about complementarianism. We need to sort out what is tradition and what is Scripture. We need to have a new conversation with text and tradition.

14. Taking the Pulse of the Study Group

On March 29, 2016, the study group for the first time took a straw poll of how its members felt about the four questions initially posed to the group. Keep in mind that the study group had been appointed as a representative cross section of the church without knowledge of where anyone stood on the issues in advance. By this point, six months into the study, only a few people had made their sentiments clearly known. So this was a big-reveal night. The results were as follows.

- **Limitations on deacon service and other leadership roles with respect to LGBT-identified members.** Fourteen group members desired that Wilshire not place limitations on deacon service and other leadership roles. One member was in favor of limitations, two were OK with LGBT members as leaders but with a limitation of celibacy, and one was undecided.
- **Limitations on ordination to ministry with respect to LGBT-identified members.** Twelve group members wanted no such limitations on ordination, five wanted limitations of celibacy, and one was unsure.
- **Limitations on same-sex marriages performed at Wilshire or officiated by staff.** Eleven group members favored no limitations on same-sex marriages at Wilshire or officiated by Wilshire's staff. Three favored limitations, three desired limitations in the church but not for weddings outside the church, and one was unsure.
- **Limitations on baby dedications for families with same-sex parents.** Thirteen group members favored no limitations on baby dedications at Wilshire when the family had same-sex parents, two wanted limitations, and three were undecided.

In hindsight, the die was cast by this straw poll, yet the study group continued to work for another three months before finalizing a recommendation. Why? Because the group continued to hold out hope that there was a way to bridge the gap and bring more people along. This struggle was captured by one member who explained to two others, "Your mind is not going to change, no matter how much we debate. [His] mind is not going to change, no matter how much we debate. The question is, How do we keep both of you in the same church?"

It is no exaggeration to say that study group members agonized over this problem. Even knowing where each individual fell in the range of opinions, there remained a burning desire to find middle ground, any middle ground. At the same time, most of the traditionalists could not escape their reading of the Bible as condemning same-sex relations, and most of the progressives could not escape their reading of the Bible as calling for unconditional love.

By this time, it was Holy Week. One of the study group members wrote to the group about this experience:

> This is how I found myself in the darkness Thursday night during our annual Maundy Thursday service, still grappling with how our church should respond. We came to the point in the service where the story of the Last Supper was read. As the words were spoken, it was as if I was hearing them for the first time. Jesus says, "A new command I give you: Love one another. As I have loved you, so must you love one another. By this everyone will know that you are my disciples, if you love one another."
>
> As I walked to receive Communion, I paused to look around the room. I saw each person reaching for the bread and the cup through a new lens with a newfound clarity. This issue for me is not about Scripture; it isn't even about individual people or who is right or wrong. For me, it is about being Jesus's disciple and loving one another.
>
> When we as a church do not allow someone the same

membership opportunities that we afford every other member, we are not loving one another as Jesus loved us. We are creating two different categories of church membership and/or Christianity. Wilshire has had different categories of church membership in her history previously. And each time we've looked at these issues (divorce, female deacons, baptism), we as a church have come to the revelation that those categories don't and shouldn't limit our membership. It is my heartfelt, prayer-guided belief that Wilshire should do the same as it relates to our Christian LGBTQ brothers and sisters. Jesus's love and grace did not come in categories. It came for *all.*

You may argue that we are showing Jesus's love by lovingly setting boundaries. I respectfully disagree. We are instead, through our actions, singling out a particular group of people as being more 'wrong' than our particular 'wrong.' Our current policy inadvertently tells LBGTQ Christians they are not equally worthy of the love and grace Jesus freely (and repetitively) pours down upon us.

This sentiment would become the majority view of the study group.

15. Majority versus Minority

We never held any expectation that the study group would reach unanimous agreement on the questions put before us. We did hope to generate some kind of consensus, with the far-fetched hope that some middle ground could be identified.

In crafting a final report, the study group originally intended to produce a single document that gave both the majority and minority views. After a noble attempt at a first draft, that plan became untenable. Those in the minority believed the single document gave short shrift to their dissent, and those in the majority believed the two positions should not be presented with equal standing.

Some in the minority wanted to present the congregation with two options to vote their convictions the way we choose between two political candidates: vote for option A or option B. Those in the majority resisted this idea because, they reasoned, the study group had been appointed to make a recommendation, not to outline choices as if there were no consensus among the group.

Underneath all this was the problem of what action the minority position would have asked the church to take. Remember, our bylaws contained no restrictions related to sexual orientation or gender identity or who could be married. (Our state denominational body, the Baptist General Convention of Texas, had been urging churches to add exclusive language into their bylaws to avoid this very conundrum.)

Outside the study group, most traditionalists were not advocating for adding restrictive language to our bylaws; what they most wanted was to have an unspoken understanding, like they believed we already had. Thus, the conserving position was to do nothing at all, to maintain the status quo. This explains the following exchange that occurred between the primary author of the majority report and the primary author of the minority report, prompting comment from others as well:

Majority author: "What is not clear to me is what it is the minority would have the church do. On page 1, you say we believe the current position of the church should not be changed; then the last page says there should be limitations. What is the current position of the church? I'm not sure you could get people to clearly articulate what that is."

Minority author: "Yes, we have struggled with that."

Another member of the minority report: "The first sentence should be changed to reflect the last sentence. Our response is that there should be limitations."

Minority author: "There has been a long-standing belief that marriage is between a man and a woman and homosexuality is sinful. When we joined, we thought the position was the same as it is at other Baptist churches. That was the assumption, but it was a false assumption on our part."

Another member of the majority report: "Was it false? There has never been any formal decision made on this thing. There has been a perception that there is a change in people's minds on this over time. From the roundtable dialogues, we did get a sense that there has been a change of view in a lot of people's minds. The purpose of this group is to clarify the church's position."

Appointed representatives of the majority and minority positions continued to work on drafting their reports, which were passed among the full group for review and comment.

The second-to-last meeting of the study group—held on June 6, 2016—was easily the most contentious meeting of the eighteen months. At this meeting, the first separate draft of a minority report was presented for discussion. And as frustrated as the minority voices had been with the original combined report, those in the majority group felt similar frustration with the minority draft. Emotions ran high, and voices were raised.

The first bone of contention was defining who was being "discriminatory" and who was being "nondiscriminatory." An original draft of the majority report had included a reference to being "nondiscriminatory," and the minority responded to that defensively.

Said one member of the minority group: "The majority report implies the nondiscriminatory stance. That's something we take offense to. It warrants being defended in our report."

Member of majority: "It adds a criterion of judgment that the majority does not."

Minority voice: "The majority view has judgment. You say if you're (coupled but) not married, you won't be ordained."

Majority voice: "The difference is one has added sexual orientation or gender identity as a limiting factor."

Another minority voice: "It's not orientation that we're counting against someone; it's behavior."

Conversation then ensued about why the minority voices were feeling so defensive.

One of the minority members: "You have a lot of work to do if you don't want the minority to feel defensive. To know that there's not one minister on our staff who agrees with the minority view makes us question everything that is said. We're wondering what words and phrases mean." Examples were cited of words and phrases in sermons by our senior pastor and prayers I had given in worship.

Finally, in exasperation, a member of the minority declared, "I'm tired. I'm tired of defending you [George and Mark]. There is a perception among people in the minority view that they are not valued and respected."

Members of the majority view were asked to explain what they found so offensive about the minority draft. Answers included the following:

- "It was hard for me to read. The current version is less offensive, more like I'm genuinely hearing your viewpoint. The first version felt harsh."
- "Some of the Scripture citations felt manipulative. I looked up every one of them, and about half are not relevant."
- "I kept wondering, 'What would I be thinking if I were [the

mother of a gay son] reading this document?' . . . At first, I didn't get your view, but now I do. I understand that you are coming from a place of love, but that's not what I read in this document. It does not appear to be coming from a place of love."

Once again, the strain between tradition and experience, between historic interpretation of Scripture and contemporary movements of the Spirit, came into sharp focus. One member of the minority referenced a statement previously made by our senior pastor that some of the less-restrictive interpretations of Scripture were "biblically plausible and theologically responsible."

"That's the best you can get to?" he asked. "That's why I can't do that."

To which our pastor replied, "We have a desire for certainty sometimes that we're not going to find. Part of my struggle with people on the Left and the Right both is they pretend to have certainty about things that are not defensible. Your argument about interpreting those biblical passages is plausible; my argument is, too. We don't always have certainty on everything. In this case, we have to go to the existential nature of what we see before us. Does my experience with this gay person look like that passage? If these are plausible arguments, we have a responsibility to be the kind of Christian community that makes judgments under the Holy Spirit's guidance. If certainty is the answer, we're not going to get there."

He noted that the minority report "gave very short shrift to the experience question," yet the reality of the pastoral life is to struggle within the tension of Scripture, tradition, and experience. "I live with this," he said. "This is my work. I'm the one who has to stand there and carry out the policies of the church, to talk to people, to their mothers, so for me, this is an existential matter."

This was followed by another member of the majority: "Five years ago, I would have been helping you write the minority report. . . . All of us with our kids and with each other start talking about Jesus as if he's a concept. Jesus isn't a concept; Jesus is a real someone who holds up his end of the relationship. We've learned this is incredibly complicated; if you've met one gay person, you've met one gay person. Our job is to introduce people to Jesus. We can't really introduce people who might really need Jesus if they won't come because they don't feel welcome. I can't tell you for sure what those verses mean, but when it gets down to our role as a church and Jesus, then the word *plausible* is OK with me."

Likewise, the minority group's explained why they had been put in a seemingly untenable position: "Sadly, accepting the majority position would put those of us in the minority in the uncomfortable position of endorsing something we sincerely believe is sinful. None of us in either the minority or the majority view believe that endorsing sin is loving. If it is sinful, then it is not good for us. The difference between the majority and the minority is that we believe Scripture teaches marriage is between a man and a woman."

16. Reporting to the Congregation

In late June 2016, the week of the much-watched Republican National Convention, our study group sent its report to the deacon officers and subsequently to the church at large. That the 2016 presidential election and our report and vote overlapped in this way should not be ignored. The matchup was unintentional, but separating the emotions of the two things may have been impossible.

Our study group chair wrote to the deacons, "The majority report of the Study Group recommends to the deacon body that we as a congregation affirm—not change—our existing bylaws, which currently contain no limitations regarding sexual orientation or gender identity. It is only by unwritten practice that Wilshire has in the past precluded leadership service by persons who identified within the LGBT spectrum, if such preclusions have actually happened at all. To the best of our knowledge, there has not yet been any request for a same-sex wedding at Wilshire or for the dedication of a baby parented by a same-sex couple. However, we fully anticipate that such requests will be made in the future, and therefore it is important for church leadership to have thought about this now."

The majority report did offer suggested language for a statement of intent, which later was dropped by the deacons and not presented to the church. That statement would have said, "Wilshire Baptist Church is called to minister equally to all persons, extending to them the privileges afforded to any follower of Christ, including, but not limited to, membership, leadership, ordination, and marriage, and will not differentiate among members on any basis save for spiritual fitness."

The report referenced four models of understanding same-sex attraction within the church and culture, which had been presented at the information sessions. They were labeled as Viewpoints A, B, C, and D and are summarized as follows:

- **Viewpoint A** sees same-sex attraction as disordered desire that must be changed if one is to experience salvation and inclusion in the church. This view sees the cause of same-sex attraction as most likely environmental (i.e., choice) and believes same-sex attraction can be corrected or cured. Under Viewpoint A, not only is same-sex behavior sinful, but same-sex attraction is sinful as well.

- **Viewpoint B** sees same-sex attraction as not sinful in and of itself but as something that must be controlled by spiritual discipline. This view maintains a sexual ethic of celibacy before marriage and faithfulness in marriage as applicable to all people, but with marriage being defined uniquely as a union between one male and one female. Those experiencing same-sex attraction may be faithful to Christ by remaining single and celibate throughout the course of their lives. In accordance with Viewpoint B, the church should teach that sexual relations are intended by God only in heterosexual relationships sealed by the covenant of marriage.

- **Viewpoint C** is grounded on the premise that most people who experience same-sex attraction have not chosen to be that way but believe this is an orientation that is given to them in their created nature. Based both on experience and a careful reading of the Bible, homosexuality is seen as sinful only when it violates the same standards of sexual activity that would apply to heterosexuals—that is, sexual relations outside of a monogamous, committed relationship.

- **Viewpoint D** does not give the same credence to biblical authority as the other views, and it would leave same-sex attraction to be addressed in whatever way the individual wishes without boundaries imposed by the church. This view might allow for having more than one open romantic relationship at a time.

The majority report reported its belief that the majority of Wilshire's members would fall somewhere between Viewpoints B and C. And then this explanation: "It bears noting that in the past, Wilshire—like most Baptist churches in America—would have primarily been populated with the A and B viewpoints. Advancements in understanding medical science and genetics, and increasing experience with friends and family members who identify within the LGBT spectrum, have worked to shift the balance within the congregation to a more centrist position. No members of the Study Group have expressed identity with Viewpoint A or Viewpoint D."

Within this framework, then, the majority of the Study Group concluded that Viewpoint C most nearly reflects biblical teaching and leads to the appropriate Christian response today.

On the matter of Scripture, the majority report noted, "A majority of the Study Group believes that the biblical texts most often cited as condemning homosexuality may or should be interpreted as prohibitions against excessive lust, abusive relationships, pederasty, and prostitution, reflecting the culture and context of the time that the Scriptures were written. These prohibitions should be honored and not ignored. Interpretations from respected theologians have supported the thinking that these texts do not address or prohibit the kind of loving same-sex relations known in our culture today."

The minority report aligned itself with Viewpoint B, concluding that all same-sex behavior in all contexts is sinful and that biblical prohibitions are clear and conclusive.

This gap between Viewpoint B and Viewpoint C also came to be illustrated by an interesting theological parsing with a history in our denominational past. From its founding in 1951 until 2000, Wilshire was affiliated with the Southern Baptist Convention (SBC). What finally pushed the church to disassociate with the SBC was forced conformity to a revised doctrinal statement, called *The Baptist Faith and Message*. Wilshire adhered and still adheres to the 1963 version of that statement; expanded portions of it are posted on the church's website under the heading "What We Believe."

One of the most controversial revisions made by the SBC in 2000 was to remove this single sentence when describing biblical interpretation: "The criterion by which the Bible is to be interpreted is Jesus Christ." The updated version instead says, "All Scripture is a testimony to Christ, who is himself the focus of divine revelation."

The sentiment of that removed line—in its full context—resides on Wilshire's website as a statement of our beliefs: "The Bible is the supreme theological determinant of our beliefs. All creeds or statements of belief, including this one, are secondary to, and should be examined in light of, Scripture. *The appropriate lens through which we understand Scripture is the life and ministry of Jesus Christ. Scripture cannot be interpreted independently of either Jesus Christ or the guidance of the Holy Spirit*" (emphasis added).

Surprisingly, the two sides of this interpretive coin became a focal point of disagreement between the majority report and the minority report. Here's how the majority report put it: "The minority report appears to be most heavily focused on the first sentence of the above-quoted distinctive. The majority fully subscribes to the first sentence but looks to the last two sentences to guide and direct the discernment process. We have concluded that the overall trajectory of the life and ministry of Jesus Christ is one of redemption and inclusion rather than one of judgment and exclusion. The Jesus we know from Scripture reached out to the marginalized and the outcast. Would he not act in a similar fashion if he were confronted with our questions?"

And here's how the minority report put it: "We strongly agree with the majority group that Christians should follow the example of Christ and reach out to 'the marginalized and the outcast.' However, we do not see it as logical that his ministry was one of redemption but not judgment, since these two principles work together. Without judgment there would be no need for redemption (John 5:22). Jesus's love was characterized by mercy beyond our human understanding, but it did not overlook or approve of sin. Rather, Jesus's ministry was all about redeeming us from the bonds of sin."

For the minority, this meant any biblical injunction against same-sex relations would be a deal breaker, regardless of the interpretive lens of the life of Jesus Christ. The report continued, "If homosexual behavior in any context is a sin, then Jesus would not want us to embrace it any more than he would want us to embrace any other sin. We should not 'cast stones,' but we must point people to the truth of Scripture and the power of God for us to live in freedom from sin."

What emerged at the end of the process was a fundamental disagreement on how to read and interpret Scripture and what sources of authority would be given what weight. Such disagreements are nothing new to the church universal, and any attempt to discuss LGBTQ inclusion might run through these waters.

To illustrate, the minority report said, "In our view, Scripture does not offer sufficient evidence to support changing the belief that marriage is intended to be between one man and one woman. We are not persuaded by the arguments set forth by the majority. Although their view might seem more compassionate and culturally acceptable, this position is inconsistent with the overarching narrative of Scripture and the ministry of Christ. In our view, the Bible is completely consistent on this matter. Our desire is to trust that God's view as revealed by Scripture is the most loving position."

The preceding paragraphs have delved into some of the finer points of the majority and minority reports, which together with an introductory letter, a pastoral response from the senior pastor, and a question-and-answer section ran thirty-five pages long. How many members actually read the full report, I can't guess. We are a well-educated congregation; one Gallup survey we did the year after the vote found that more than 50 percent of our members hold graduate degrees. Yet wading through all the documentation of the study group and its recommendations surely was too much for more than a few people.

Where is the line between just enough information and too much information on a difficult subject? Looking back, I still don't know the answer to that question. In the end, the decision boiled down to some sound-bite messages, just as in the national political campaign that was swirling around us at the time.

When the deacons received the study group's reports, they discussed and debated at length. And then they authorized the chair of deacons to notify the congregation that there would be a vote on a resolution from the deacons. That notice went out on October 18, 2016.

The resolution had been approved by the deacons on a 47–3 vote and was described as "the best way to serve the church and bring us together." It stated, "RESOLVED, *that the membership of Wilshire Baptist Church affirms its existing bylaws, which provide for a single class of membership.*" In case there was any confusion, the deacons also provided interpretation of what this vote meant:

- **By voting YES on the resolution,** the membership affirms the bylaws, which provide for one class of membership. Therefore, this resolution would permit all members to participate in congregational life on the same basis as any other church member regardless of sexual orientation or gender identity. This affirms the ability of the church's committees and lay and staff governance structures to consider all members for leadership, ordination, baby dedication, and marriage based upon individual merit and the discernment of those duly elected to governance positions.
- **By voting NO on the resolution**, the membership affirms the existing operational principle that does not allow some members to be considered for certain leadership roles, ordination, baby dedication, and marriage based upon sexual orientation or gender identity.

At that deacons' meeting, Senior Pastor George Mason gave some of the most emotional comments of his then-twenty-seven-year tenure at Wilshire. "I wish I had magic," he said. "I wish I were a good enough pastor who could find the right words to move us forward and be together. But I don't have that. The alternatives of being together and doing nothing or moving forward and not being together are the only ways to be."

17. We Love Wilshire

Looking back on what happened that I and other leaders had failed to anticipate, two things stand out: First, I did not expect that a loyal opposition group would form and engage in campaign-style tactics such as direct-mail pieces, phone trees, email groups, and organizing rides to the church to vote. Second, I did not anticipate that I would come to coin the phrase "viral discontent."

Here's what I mean by viral discontent: On any contentious issue within a church, it only takes one or two influential negative voices to sow seeds of discontent that can quickly take hold among their peers. These key influencers have the potential to change the course of the conversation, regardless of how well thought out it may have been, or even to shut down a healthy conversation.

We lost more people than anticipated over this vote for one simple reason: viral discontent. We lost people we shouldn't have lost because the friends they had known and loved for years became so angry about the decision facing the church that they infected the spirits of everyone around them with negativity. And this kind of negativity is never just about the one presenting issue; in church fights, it is always like a snowball rolling down a hill, gathering every flake of discontent and previous slights that can congeal together.

Suddenly, we heard members expressing disappointment over everything from our 1991 decision to ordain women to our more recent foray into advocating against payday lenders. Perceived slights of long-term members not invited to serve on previous committees, of family members who had left over other issues, and of disagreement over the management of investments all got bundled up together. Thus, for some, the decision to become inclusive of the LGBTQ community was the last straw or the bridge too far.

What we previously had celebrated as a healthy diversity within the congregation immediately began to fracture. And like rocks tumbling off a mountain in a landslide, key influencers began to pull others in their wake as they planned an exit. For a few, it was not enough to be upset themselves; they needed to make others upset with them. And for a very few, it was not enough to leave the church; they wanted to take the whole thing down as they walked out the door.

Those extremes were not the norm, however, even among the longtime members who eventually parted ways over the LGBTQ vote. The vast majority of people who left did so graciously and with genuine remorse. But in almost every case, I can draw a line from them to someone else who stoked the flames of fear in them. That's the power of viral discontent.

By the way, viral discontent may also originate outside the system. For example, family members who don't even live in Dallas held tremendous sway over some of our members who left. There were parents who threatened their adult children with what would happen if their grandchildren attended a church where they might have a gay Sunday school teacher. Adult siblings shamed their brothers or sisters about being part of such a liberal church.

Some of the absolute saddest departures for me were church members who on their own would have been fine staying after the vote but who were so entangled with friends or family members that they felt they really had no choice but to leave. It turned out that maintaining long-standing friendships rose above all other concerns.

Another form of viral discontent was created, perhaps unintentionally, by the organization of a loyal opposition group that called itself "We Love Wilshire." That name, of course, didn't set well with the rest of the church, who believed that they, too, loved Wilshire and that neither side had a corner on love for the church.

One lifelong member in favor of inclusion remarked on this at the later church conference: "I know most of the people who signed the 'We Love Wilshire' letter. I speak for the other half of Wilshire and say, 'We love Wilshire, too.' We are dealing with a question that once asked can't be ignored."

I am convinced that most of the motivation for forming this opposition effort was pure and without malice. For some, this was the only apparent way to save their beloved church from fracture. The motivation was, indeed, love. For others, this simply became a political strategy no different from the state and local and national political campaigns playing out at the same time.

The first hint of what was going on came with a phone call from a lifelong member of the church who wanted me to reserve space for him to prepare an all-church mailing and for me to provide him with a mailing list of every member of the church. That immediately prompted a search of the church bylaws to see whether I could accommodate either of those things.

As it turns out, the bylaws are specific yet vague, allowing that members may "inspect" the church roll but offering no provision for wholesale copying of the membership roll or being given mailing labels. After consulting with the deacon officers, I was able to provide the requested space and allow a few representatives of We Love Wilshire to come to my office and "inspect" the rolls. They did so over a period of two hours, calling out to each other in an assembly line fashion of comparing their copied versions of a church directory against the official roll.

From this inspection, a letter went out to the entire congregation, signed by individuals from 100 households. Later, a second letter went out with additional signatures, 212 individuals in all.

Here are the two most difficult parts of the signature pages on those two mailings: Not everyone who signed understood what they were signing, as not all had been given an opportunity to read the text of the letters in advance. And some who lent their names mainly out of fear of a church split found themselves after the vote wondering if they could stay in the church and let others know they were not angry or even upset. Several dear friends who came to my adult Sunday school class sheepishly asked me if they would be welcomed, because, "you know, we signed the letter." To which my response was "Yes, absolutely."

The first letter, which went out before the deacons considered the reports from the study group, urged members to contact deacons to oppose the majority report. The pastor later told deacons he believed this campaign was "unprecedented" in the church's history.

That four-page letter, filled with underlined passages and numbered lists and italics, warned that if the recommendation of the study group were implemented, Wilshire would be removed from membership in the Baptist General Convention of Texas and lose our historic identity as a Texas Baptist church. And it reasoned that things were fine just as they always had been, quoting the maxim "If it ain't broke, don't fix it."

The second We Love Wilshire letter stated its intent to "demonstrate to the leadership that the church is so divided on this issue that it would be unwise to push for a vote now." This letter was sent after the deacons had voted 47–3 to call for a congregational vote. It continued, "Apparently, forcing a division in the church just does not make any difference to those who want the new policies." Then the letter gave five reasons members should oppose the deacon-recommended resolution:

1. Wilshire will become a smaller church.
2. Wilshire will become a poorer church.
3. Wilshire will become a more isolated church.
4. Wilshire members will become suspicious of what may come next.
5. The intent of the resolution is inappropriately ambiguous.

Response to the two all-church mailings was swift and angry. Members who favored the deacon resolution and some who were neutral or undecided on the matter began writing letters and emails addressed to the We Love Wilshire email address and post office box. The fact that a group of members would organize in such a blatantly political effort was incomprehensible to those who thought of our congregation as a lovable Mayberry.

Here's a sampling of comments that were sent simultaneously to the church office or to deacon officers:

- "I understand that many people in the We Love Wilshire group have been members for multiple generations. It truly makes me sad that they would be willing to leave this long history over a decision that will probably never impact them directly. But just because you've been here a long time and given large sums of money doesn't give you a larger voice."

- "I believe 'We all love Wilshire' is a stretch, given how many members have already abandoned ship. It's hard to express one's love for Wilshire and a desire to carry out its mission when one chooses not to attend."

- "I, too, love Wilshire, and I am deeply disturbed by your letter. It may be that this is an election year and partisanship is in the air, but to me it sounds more political than spiritual."

- "Viewing the names who signed the We Love Wilshire letter both broke my heart and infuriated me. There are some on the list that I've never heard speak a word until now. Now they are incensed. Some have taken their money and already left Wilshire but still fear enough to want to influence the outcome. This is unethical at best. Others, I pray will remain, so we can worship under the same roof like we always have."

- "It is my hope and prayer that the deacon body of Wilshire will stand up to this bullying and narrative of fear and that you all will help lead our congregation in the loving and inclusive spirit of Jesus."

- "While I understand the emotions and concerns that the diversity initiative has aroused at Wilshire, I was saddened by the recent letter challenging the church efforts in addressing the issue. Although the intent may have been well-meaning, the result was a derisive, incendiary, polarizing screed. Sprinkled with false assumptions, half-truths, and hints of conspiracy, it did little to advance the dialogue that has been going on for the past year. To many of us, including my family, it was a personally painful attack on our faith and spiritual community."

- "I am so saddened by your letter and disappointed by the names on it. Not because we differ in opinion, but because you would sign your name to a document, one that some of you have admitted to not reading first, which is designed to be a scare tactic at best, and at worst, to implode our community of faith."

No doubt the organizers of We Love Wilshire also received affirming communications, but those typically were not shared with me or church leadership. It would be accurate to say that the We Love Wilshire mailings produced far more backlash than the organizers could have imagined or intended. And it encouraged the progressives and undecideds in the congregation to show up and vote.

18. Church Conference

After the deacons approved the recommendation to the church, an all-church conference was scheduled in multiple parts. The first part was a Sunday noon open forum, where members could speak for or against the recommendation to have one class of membership. The second part would be the two Sundays of voting, at the conclusion of both morning services on two consecutive weeks.

At the open forum, tensions ran high. The first person to speak was a matriarch of the church, ninety-five years old. Although supportive of her pastor, she and he were "poles apart in this decision," she said. "We strongly disagree, and I am not voting for this."

However, rather than lobbying voters to side with her, she encouraged everyone to vote their convictions and then stay around to do the hard work of being church together. "If you really love Wilshire, vote your conviction, but regardless of the results, after the vote, I will be here, and I hope you will stay with me and keep Wilshire the same vibrant church it has always been. Let's accept the results and work together as Christians and make this the strongest church that we can. . . . Please do not go off and leave. I will be here as long as I am able."

Sadly, of the members who made public declarations about how Wilshire would always be their church despite the outcome of the vote, she was one of the few who actually stayed after the vote went the other way. One of the saddest reminders in researching this book has been to see over and over the faithful members who declared their undying love for the church despite the outcome of the vote yet left the next week after their views lost.

Not much new ground was plowed in the nearly two-hour forum. Prepared speeches were made, but few minds were changed. Neither side did a good job of presenting a case.

One older man expressed the views of many of his peers who were concerned that their opposition to the recommendation would label them as "bigots" or "haters." He explained, "I don't want us to be a community that calls each other bigots or haters. I fear Wilshire is moving into that movement of deceitful accusations. I urge you not to fear these accusations, but let the loving community we know as Wilshire prevail."

This pushed at one of the hardest questions communities have to address in discussing inclusion versus exclusion: Where is the line defining who is a bigot? Few people want to be labeled as such, yet sometimes those who fear the label actually meet the definition.

Just a few weeks before this church forum, one of our pastoral residents (young clergy in post-seminary practicum) had been challenged in this man's adult Bible study class. This staff member, who is black, was asked to explain to the room full of white senior adults "why black people have so many special privileges white people don't have." This happened in an otherwise theologically progressive church that has been deeply involved in working toward racial conciliation. To our black staff member, that felt like bigotry plain and simple.

Keep in mind once again that this all was playing out in the fall of 2016, when no one thought Donald Trump would win the presidency and when few of us understood the depth of latent racism even within the Christian church. In my mind, these two issues—racism and homophobia—are too often intertwined.

In fairness, opponents of our decision to open the church to full inclusion of the LGBTQ community would disagree with the statement just made. They would tell you that sexual orientation is not like race, because in their view, race is not something you choose, but sexual orientation is. One member of our study group explained it this way: "Homosexuality is different than issues of race and gender and slavery in the New Testament in that it is always condemned but these other issues are not. On the issue of gentiles, the early church had to look back at the Old Testament and saw there that God had intended all along to include gentiles. Thus, there were plenty of texts in Scripture that would lend support to a gentile mission, but there are not texts like that to support homosexuality."

Yet the arguments made against LGBTQ inclusion sound a lot like the arguments made against racial integration a generation ago. For example, one of the opponents of LGBTQ inclusion said at the church forum, "I am voting no because I am a lifelong Bible-believing Baptist and don't intend to change. That is what we are doing with this vote; we are changing. For some, it is a good thing, but not this, not here, not now. The Bible can never mean what it never meant."

Christians often attempt a perceived middle ground by parsing the difference between loving the sinner and hating the sin. An example is this statement from the open forum: "Is it really our desire to question the Bible's condemnation of sin? Jesus loves all people, and he also condemns their sin. If we love and embrace the person and love and embrace the sin, is that loving the person as Christ loves them?" Or consider this statement: "I don't want people to think that because I am against this, I don't love them. I welcome those who aren't straight. All have sinned and fall short of the glory of God. I have my own sins but not this one. I am not here to judge one over another."

Christians who identify within the LGBTQ community hear these "compromises" as merely another form of condemnation, an "I love you, but . . ." From their perspective, "sin" is something you can choose not to do, and being attracted to persons of the same sex is how they are made, not what they choose to do. Lust is something you can choose not to follow, whether you're gay or straight. But sexual orientation is not a sin like gluttony or envy or pride.

This line of reasoning often brings the debate back to science, even for those who will always choose the Bible over a scientific study. Thus this statement at the open forum: "I believe science is not conclusive that people are born LGBT. I do not know why we as a church are disregarding Scripture. The Old and New Testaments were inspired by God. The Scripture is clear in Leviticus that you are not to have sex with someone of the same gender."

On the other side, members mainly appealed to emotion and intuition, which, as previously noted, drives traditionalists crazy.

Exemplary was this well-intended statement: "I want my children and grandchildren to remember me as someone who loves unconditionally and nonjudgmentally. I would accept my grandchildren unconditionally, no matter what path they choose. Love is my guide on this and not to judge from where I have not walked."

The most interesting thing to happen that afternoon was that four teenagers had the courage to stand before the capacity crowd and voice their support for full inclusion. "I grew up Christian," one said. "'Christian' means love. If we oppose this, I feel it will change some of the younger views on what Christianity means. I am against people being denied privileges due to sexual orientation." And this from another teenager: "I want to be part of a church that loves everyone unconditionally. If you don't accept it now, maybe you can grow to accept it."

19. The Vote and the Fallout

We couldn't have chosen a worse time to schedule a vote on such a difficult issue. Our churchwide vote occurred on two Sundays—the ones just before and just after the 2016 presidential election. That happened to be the way the calendar fell if we were to settle the issue before Advent.

One of the great unknown questions in my mind is whether the outcome would have been any different if the timing had been different. Would the church have been less divided if the country had been less divided? Two years later, I posed this question to two friends—one a lifelong Republican who with great remorse had left our church after the vote and one a younger Democrat who was in favor of full inclusion and stayed. Both of them thought my question missed the mark, but for different reasons.

The Republican, a senior adult who is a fiscal conservative but not a social conservative, said he honestly never had thought about a connection between our discussion and the national presidential cycle. He thought for what seemed like a long time before responding, citing instead three other reasons why most who left had done so. When I pressed him to ask if older conservatives like him might have seen the action of the church as just more evidence of encroaching liberalism in all of American society, he said that could have been possible, but if so, he was not aware of it at the time.

The Democrat, a political moderate who works in the business world, said he thinks it is highly likely that political conservatives could have seen LGBTQ inclusion as part of a broader breakdown of society. But having our church conversation earlier in the year before the election would not have changed the outcome, he said, because for months, the conventional wisdom was that Hillary Clinton would win the race. There was no point during the run-up to Election Day when conservatives felt less threatened. However, having the church vote after the election might have made the vote for inclusion more overwhelming, due to the backlash of progressives and centrists against the perceived threat of the election outcome.

Again, we'll never know for sure how these two events connected in the minds of our church members. I have to believe there was at least some overlap.

Another outside force more clearly influenced our process. The week before our vote began, the leader of the Baptist General Convention of Texas sent us a letter that was a shot across the bow perceived internally as an attempt to influence our decision from outside. And in so doing, he stirred up a media storm we had hoped to avoid but that turned out to be a blessing in disguise.

A bit of background is necessary here for those not versed in Baptist polity and particularly in the uniqueness of Baptists in Texas. Wilshire was founded in 1951 and immediately affiliated with the Southern Baptist Convention (SBC) and the Baptist General Convention of Texas (BGCT). In those days, the state and national bodies were inextricably linked but with the pretense of autonomy, which is a cherished Baptist principle. The only notable difference between the two denominational bodies then was geography.

Beginning in 1979, the SBC took a sharp rightward turn, in what came to be known as "the controversy" or "the fundamentalist takeover of the SBC" or "the conservative resurgence," depending on your point of view. The BGCT and Wilshire were among those who opposed the rightward shift, which required more and more forced conformity. Ultimately, Wilshire left the SBC in 2000 and focused exclusively on its partnership with the Cooperative Baptist Fellowship, a breakaway group from the SBC that began in 1991. But we also remained in good standing with the Texas Baptist group.

Texas Baptists so opposed what was going on in the SBC that the right flank of the state body split off in 1998 to form their own state convention more loyal to the national body. In theory, that should have left the original state body more comfortable with a theologically progressive identity, but that was not to be the case. Instead, the state convention spent years trying to staunch the flow of any more churches defecting to the new convention—thus becoming hypersensitive to any concern expressed from the Right and ultimately taking for granted the support that always had been there from the Left.

After nearly twenty years of this fear-based existence, a vocal group within Texas Baptists homed in on same-sex relations and same-sex marriage as the line in the sand that could not be crossed. The BGCT executive board in February 2015 unanimously adopted a resolution asserting that gender is determined biologically, not psychologically.[1] This issue was driven by some of the Texas Baptist–affiliated universities that opposed having to make housing accommodations for transgender students. The resolution declared that "in creation, God made male and female as biological gender assignment." It expressed "great concern with the emergence of the transgender agenda and the notion that one's gender is determined psychologically, not biologically."

This followed a multiyear pattern of BGCT leadership and governing bodies acting against churches that crossed the line on LGBTQ acceptance. In 2010, Texas Baptists excluded Royal Lane Baptist Church in Dallas when it ordained gay deacons and published on its website its openness to the LGBTQ community. That followed a precedent set in 1998, when the BGCT executive board removed University Baptist Church in Austin for ordaining a gay deacon and publishing that action on its website.[2]

So we should not have been surprised to learn that Texas Baptist leaders had their eyes set on Wilshire and would act swiftly to remove us, too, if we crossed the line. Except that we had taken great pains to be in constant communication with BGCT staff and elected leadership and hoped to be proactive in finding a way to work together in the future.

The truth is that the BGCT needed us more than we needed them. On the one hand, we received no financial support from the state

---

1. Leah Reynolds, "BGCT Executive Board Approves Resolution on Transgender Issues," Baptist General Convention of Texas, February 26, 2015, https://tinyurl.com/y8lxvx8t.
2. Ken Camp, "Board Distances BGCT from Gay-Affirming Dallas Church," Baptist News Global, May 25, 2010, https://tinyurl.com/ybkt4sv6.

convention, no leadership support—nothing other than identity and a conduit to support missions work. On the other, Wilshire historically was a top financial contributor to the work of Texas Baptists and consistently was the number-one or number-two contributor in the state to the Texas Baptist Offering for World Hunger.

Let this sink in for a moment: Texas Baptist leaders were so afraid of being tainted by allowing participation of an LGBTQ-affirming congregation that they were willing to turn away tens of thousands of dollars in contributions to an annual offering to help feed hungry people around the world. Once removed from the state convention, we were not allowed to send money to their causes, even if we asked for no representation in return. Texas Baptists said they valued purity on LGBTQ exclusion more than feeding hungry people.

We did everything possible to remain supportive of the BGCT, even if its leaders could not support us. We were fine with a one-way relationship for the sake of feeding hungry children and supporting other gospel causes. Our senior pastor had proposed a way for us and churches like us to remain in fellowship through a kind of "watch care" status. That was rejected by BGCT leadership, and we were voted out quickly. Let this be clear: we did not leave the BGCT willingly; we were kicked out.

And the threat of being kicked out was used by the BGCT executive director in a way that our folks saw as an attempt to influence our congregational vote. That didn't go down well, especially when it gave the appearance of being coordinated with the We Love Wilshire campaign.

On November 8, 2016, BGCT executive director David Hardage sent Wilshire a letter warning, "Should your church choose to publicly affirm same-sex sexual behavior, the BGCT will no longer be able to accept funds from the church, seat its messengers to the annual meeting, allow the church to express affiliation with the BGCT or allow its members to serve on the BGCT boards, committees or other roles."[3] He also explained the jeopardy that would befall the several BGCT employees who were members of our church: that they would have to join a different church or lose their jobs, something we already knew and had been working quietly to negotiate. This letter was sent in the week between our two Sundays of voting, and it somehow got to the press, which launched a series of reports that drew national attention to our internal deliberations.

Our senior pastor, George Mason, replied to Hardage with dismay, "I count the timing of this letter coming to our church to be unfortunate in that we are yet to complete our voting on the matter this coming Sunday. The decision to send us this information at this time may be purely coincidental and unintended, but it nonetheless amounts to an external influence over our church decision-making process that is by Baptist principle a matter of local church freedom that should not be influenced by relationships with bodies that are based solely on voluntary cooperation." He further noted that even if the congregation voted to allow full participation by those in the LGBTQ community, we would not have taken any of the specific actions previously noted by the BGCT as disqualifying. We had not ordained a gay person, conducted a same-sex marriage, or even published pro-LGBTQ-identifying statements.

Our intent had been to take a low-key approach to any statements or publicity about our vote, regardless of outcome. Those plans were dashed in a moment, not by us but by the premature action of the BGCT. From that moment forward, the press came calling, wanting to know what we were doing and why. Although frustrating, that turned out to be a tremendous gift, which will be described in the next chapter.

Most Texans don't like to be intimidated, and Baptists in Texas especially don't like to be told what to do. Folks at Wilshire felt like the BGCT executive director was out of line with his premature letter, and that only strengthened the resolve of some to vote for

---

3. Ken Camp, "Two Churches Face Removal from BGCT Due to Gay Issue," *Baptist Standard*, November 9, 2016, https://tinyurl.com/ybyqcnss.

full inclusion. Further, the irony was not lost on our well-educated members that the state Baptist convention that had once stood up to fundamentalist rigidity in the SBC now was enforcing its own kind of fundamentalist rigidity on us.

The process of voting became an elaborate system. With more than sixteen hundred active members eligible to vote and an equal number of inactive members who, in theory, could show up to vote, we needed to ensure integrity of the process. Our deacon officers and I worked together with our church clerk to produce paper ballots that were inserted into envelopes with labels for every eligible voting member. Since the bylaws required members to be physically present to vote, everyone came to a central location, where deacons staffed tables to hand out individual envelopes by name. The church clerk was on hand to resolve any problems, which were few.

Voting took place at the conclusion of each of our two morning worship services on the two designated Sundays. Those who wanted to cast a ballot had to walk to the front of the sanctuary to place their anonymous paper ballots in large boxes. After the first Sunday of voting, the ballots were immediately taken to the church safe and not counted. Counting commenced only after the final ballots had been cast.

To say that people came out of the woodwork to vote would be an understatement. We saw members at church those two Sundays we hadn't seen in years—members who, I believe, voted in both directions. We also saw a number of once-faithful members who for months had been attending another church in town (which they intended to join but purposely had not yet joined) come back as a final act of defiance to vote against the proposed full inclusion.

On the first Sunday of voting, which was All Saints Day and two days before the United States presidential election, George Mason in his sermon acknowledged the elephants in the room. "We are in an election week in our country and in our church," he said. "We will vote in both cases on matters that have divided us. We have different visions of how to fulfill our hopes and dreams, of what these communities should look like. And along the way, we have sometimes hurt one another and closed our hearts to each other. Some have determined that it is better to live without one another than with one another. Some would rather move to Canada than live in a future in our country under the administration of the one they didn't vote for. Some would rather move to another church than live under the conditions of a future determined by a vote they didn't support. But by doing so, we only prove that the way the world operates is the only way open to us."

And then he offered this pastoral word: "I am aware that this may be the last time many of us will worship together. If you are one of those who have already decided that you are leaving, I have something to say to you: thank you. Thank you for all the years of sacrifice and service. Thank you for the gifts of time, talents, and treasure that you have given to make us the church we are today. And if you wonder how you will be remembered after you leave, I will tell you: you will be recorded among the saints of this church. No one wants to be judged on the basis of one decision or snapshot of time in a life. So we will bless you and miss you."

Then he added, "And for those of you who are undecided, I want to say that there is a place for you here. It may be hard, but it can be good. A good life, not an easy life, don't you know? Let's prove the gospel together by staying together. But whether you leave or stay, don't let hatred or bitterness or resentment rule your heart."

At noon on the second Sunday of voting, a team of deacons gathered to process the ballots in a way that allowed for counting and recounting by different groups to verify the results. We had promised to notify the congregation by email that afternoon of the outcome.

The motion to affirm that the church bylaws recognize a single class of membership, regardless of sexual orientation or gender identity, passed by a 61 percent favorable vote. There were 948 ballots cast, 577 in favor, 367 not in favor, and four abstentions. While 61 percent may not sound like a landslide, consider the gap between the affirmative votes and the negative votes: twenty-two percentage points. Statistically speaking, that's huge.

George Mason interpreted this to the congregation in his after-noon email: "This is the largest voter participation in recent memory. By comparison, when the church voted in 1991 to allow for the ordination of women, there were fewer than 450 votes cast, and the motion passed by a 67 percent majority. The vote to call me as pastor of Wilshire in 1989 totaled 901 ballots cast (with a 92 percent majority). This unprecedented level of engagement is heartening in that it demonstrates at the most basic level the interest of members in seeking God's will for the church."

Then he offered these further words of understanding: "While I cannot read the minds of all who voted against the motion, I believe I know their hearts. Their greatest concern in voting no was that they be falsely cast as being unloving toward gay persons. It will be important going forward now to make clear that we trust each other's hearts and believe the best about each other. . . . Wilshire next Sunday will look much like Wilshire last Sunday. . . . Extending full privileges and equal responsibilities to LGBT Christians does not mean restricting or marginalizing anyone else, including those who disagree."

Unfortunately, he also had to address the fact that we now were in the media spotlight—something we had hoped to avoid—and had to act responsibly. The lessons learned two years prior through the Ebola crisis taught us the value of following what I call Mark's number-one rule of communication: "You're always better off telling your own story rather than letting someone else shape the story for you."

That is a lesson learned from my years as a journalist, and it is advice I frequently give to anyone who will listen. Any time a crisis hits, whatever the organization, you always fare better with the media when you are forthcoming and get ahead of the curve. Anytime you wait and get put in a reactionary mode, you've already lost. Get out there and tell your story first. In this case, the action of the BGCT had forced our hand and required us to speak.

George said to the church, "We would prefer to bear witness in our own words instead of simply having others talk about us.

Among the things we will acknowledge is that we are not alone in taking this direction. Baptist churches all over the country, many affiliated as we are with the Cooperative Baptist Fellowship, others that are former BGCT-related churches, and several local Presbyterian, Methodist, Episcopal, Lutheran, and United Church of Christ churches, to name a few, have preceded us in this journey. We are grateful for their partnership in witness to the gospel that is open to all and closed to none."

What we thought would be an internal decision that would slowly work its way out over time quickly became the talk of the town. We were on every local TV station, in the *Dallas Morning News* and the *Washington Post*.

Letters and emails started pouring in with both thanks and condemnation for our action. One of the first emails was from someone in the community, who wrote, "When I see Wilshire Baptist Church, I see the face of Jesus! I am not a member of Wilshire, nor a Baptist. I am a Christian. I have seen over the past couple of years your outreach to God's children, whether they be gay, grieving, displaced, sick (Ebola), etc. You are what I believe the Bible expects of the Christian Church."

Another nonmember wrote, "I just wanted to reach out and say thank you for showing kindness and compassion towards the LGBT community. Your actions could not have come at a better time with all of the strife in today's society. I was sadly disappointed and very frightened for my future from the recent election outcome, and your kind and welcoming gesture has renewed my faith. I truly believe God has worked his grace through you, and I did not want it to go unmentioned."

We also received emails of condemnation, including an extremely lengthy screed from an unnamed author who wrote, "Is the senior pastor at Wilshire Baptist Church desperately ignorant of the truth about LGBT health risks? . . . Fact: Gay men are full of disease, sexually transmitted diseases, HIV, infection and parasites. . . . Given the many diseases associated with homosexuality, the Bible prohibition against homosexuality is arguably one of the many examples where the Bible exhibited knowledge that was ahead of its time."

People we never met began giving us one-star reviews on our Facebook page, lecturing about the heresy of our position. This appeared to be a coordinated effort from a strict church group in another city. However, seeing these flaming reviews only prompted our members and friends to counter with positive reviews of their own.

And, sadly, resignation emails began to arrive—a few members resigning as deacons or teachers or committee members. Most departed with gracefulness and sorrow. Most painful, though, were the longtime members and friends who slipped away without even saying good-bye.

While some members walked away, outsiders made online contributions as a way of saying thanks. One such contribution came with the memo line saying simply, "Love wins."

Internally, members both celebrated and winced at the media coverage. One member who is a media professional with a large company wrote George and me to say, "Please consider not feeding further media coverage on the controversy. . . . Playing denominational politics out in the media further will hurt Wilshire's witness as well as Baptists and Christians in general." At the same time, another member reported being approached by a colleague in the workplace who had heard the news and wanted to know if this member would meet him if he and his wife came to worship at Wilshire the next Sunday.

This is the double-edged sword of publicity. And it was the same during the Ebola crisis. Some members took pride in our moment in the media, and some feared we were doing damage.

Looking back two years later, it is clear to me that the unintended publicity helped us far more than it hurt us. The growth we have experienced since the vote for inclusion was sparked by awareness of the vote for inclusion. Not making that known—as we had originally hoped—would have left us open to new members but without potential new members knowing we were open.

The Sunday after the vote, which was the first Sunday in Advent that year, ushered in a peace we could not have predicted. Our numbers were down—way down—but those who were present were happy and positive, and the tension that had been in the air for months was suddenly gone. The difference was palpable.

We got picketed that Sunday. People who didn't know us but felt ordained by God to correct the error of our ways marched up and down the sidewalk with placards and shouted hellfire and damnation.

Later that day, we discovered the sidewalk in front of the church, which faces a busy city street, had been covered in chalk writing and drawing. But this time, we received words of affirmation, including a huge central message: "Thank you for loving all people." It turns out that some of our neighbors, having witnessed the picketers that morning, determined to stage a counterprotest. They used chalk to write out messages of love and support all over the sidewalk. And the next Sunday morning, they showed up with signs of their own to praise the church and thank us. That was balm to a wounded soul, and we would need that encouragement in the days ahead.

20. Rebuilding

Here's the bottom line: Because of our decision to become fully inclusive of the LGBTQ community, we lost 275 members, about 15 percent of our active membership. Some left early in the study process, some left during the study process, and many others left immediately after the vote. Still others continued to trickle out over the next six months or more. The losses just kept mounting.

Yet at the same time, new people arrived. The number of guests in every worship service increased dramatically. Some were friends from the community who just wanted to show their support. Others were people who had been out of church for years and now were inspired to check out a church where they might find welcome.

Weekly worship attendance and Sunday-morning Bible study attendance dropped by about two hundred people from where we had been a year or two before. Many longtime members were no longer found in their normal pews. But every week, dozens of new faces appeared in the pews—often people who were not ready to fill out a guest card or to linger to talk with anyone after the service. They were too afraid, too scarred from past experiences with the church. They needed time to see if we really were going to become what we said we would.

Here's a point we failed to anticipate: Just because we opened our doors to everyone did not mean everyone would immediately trust us. We would have to earn that trust over the weeks and months ahead.

Over the first year after the vote, we gained about 130 new members. That number continued to grow in the coming months and years. In my twenty-year history with the church, I never before had seen so many new faces in the congregation. And that trend continues to this day. By November 2018, two full years after the vote, we had received more new members than the number of members we had lost over the vote.

And the demographics of the congregation changed in ways we had not anticipated. Seemingly overnight, we became a much younger church. Of the adult members we lost, 70 percent were age sixty or older; only 20 percent were under age fifty. And of the new members who came, 70 percent were under age sixty.

One of my favorite illustrations of an exception to this age differential is a senior adult couple who came to visit one Sunday. They explained they were longtime members of another large Baptist church that had received perhaps 150 of our members in the exodus. As they listened to the newcomers complain every week about why they had left Wilshire, they realized the very qualities being described sounded like a great church to them, so they had to come check it out. This couple found a new home at Wilshire and have made great new members.

What mainly regrew the church was word of mouth. We did no advertising or special emphases to declare our openness. We didn't put up rainbow flags. Other than the media coverage that came our way, we just kept on being church.

More than a year after the vote, we cosponsored a Dallas stop on the national book tour for Jen Hatmaker and Nichole Nordeman. Jen is a Christian blogger with a huge following especially among younger Christian women, and she had recently lost publishing deals because of her newfound acceptance of same-sex marriage. I got to give a brief welcome at that event, which had filled McFarlin Auditorium at Southern Methodist University with a capacity crowd of twenty-three hundred. I explained that for anyone seeking a church home that was welcoming to all people, we were such a church.

About two weeks later, a young family came to greet me after worship. The woman said, "I heard you speak at the Moxie Matters tour. You said this was a church that welcomes all people. We've come to see if that's true." They found it was true, joined the church on their second visit, and are now deeply engaged in the church. This heterosexual couple with two young children simply wanted to raise their children in a church that welcomes all people. I could repeat variations on that story over and over.

Soon after the vote, a woman who came to visit explained she really had not thought she was worthy to be part of a church. But she explained that she had watched how we handled the Ebola crisis, then the LGBT question, and she thought to herself, "If they can love other people like that, maybe they would love me, too."

A woman who was raised Catholic and felt like she had worn a big letter D on her chest since becoming divorced began visiting regularly. When we served Communion in worship, she found herself weeping. This was the first time in years she had received Communion, because she had not been allowed to partake in her own church due to her divorce.

A seminary-trained gay man who was raising a fourteen-year-old daughter came to visit in my office. He explained to me with tears in his eyes how grateful he was to have found a church where his straight daughter would be welcomed as the child of a gay man. And then he said, "I cannot believe I have found a church that believes and teaches the Bible but yet welcomes me as a gay man."

One of the first area clergy to reach out to us with an offer of help was Neil Cazares-Thomas, pastor of Cathedral of Hope in Dallas, one of the first and largest predominantly gay Christian churches in America. Neil knew what kind of backlash we likely would get, and he offered his counsel and encouragement. He quickly proposed that our two congregations do something together as a sign of Christian unity.

It took a year and a half for that to happen, but during Holy Week 2018, we shared both Maundy Thursday and Good Friday services, the first a joint event at Wilshire and the second a joint event at Cathedral of Hope. Doing so was not without controversy on our side, as some who had been barely holding on after the vote eighteen months earlier saw this as an unnecessarily provocative action.

What happened those two nights, though, was more a movement of the Spirit than I could have imagined. Our sanctuary on Maundy Thursday was flooded with perhaps two hundred or more Cathedral of Hope members, many of whom had been raised in Baptist churches but excluded later due to their sexual orientation or gender identity. They were in awe that a Baptist church would welcome them. And then on Good Friday, a smaller number of Wilshire members received the warmest welcome possible at Cathedral of Hope. When Neil introduced George Mason and said words of affirmation about Wilshire, the entire Cathedral of Hope congregation stood and gave us a lengthy standing ovation. I have seldom seen George Mason speechless, but that night he was so moved, so emotional, so dumbfounded that words were hardly possible. A church full of Christians who knew what it was like to be rejected welcomed us with an ovation.

Later that night, as we entered a quiet space to meditate upon the cross of Jesus's suffering, a senior adult friend who is the mother of a transgender child embraced me and said, "I never thought I would live to see this day." We both began weeping—I to the point of sobbing and shaking—at the realization of the holy ground on which we stood on that Good Friday at the foot of the cross.

Lest this paint too rosy a picture, understand that we continued to mourn our losses for months. Three adult Sunday school classes—including one of the largest senior adult classes—disappeared. Committees experienced the largest number of vacancies we had known before. We lost about $750,000 in contributions to our $5 million unified budget and adjusted it downward correspondingly. Somehow, we managed to retain all our staff through the transition. What suffered financially were our mission partners and special projects we had planned to fund.

One of the lessons learned through the shakeup was that we unintentionally had created silos within the church. Through our age-graded adult classes we created environments where people often had agreement among themselves and assumed others in the church shared those views. The large senior adult class that moved almost en masse to another Baptist church had been together for thirty-five to forty years or more. Even among the few class members who didn't share the majority's political and theological views, the power of long-term friendships overrode any differences.

When that class decamped to the other church, a few members were left behind and began visiting other classes for the first time in decades. What they found shocked and pleasantly surprised them. One couple said to me upon visiting my class the first time, "Is your class always this energetic and full of discussion?"

One of the lessons of rebuilding was to create more avenues for intergenerational communication and to help members understand the diversity of opinions and backgrounds within the church. This remains a challenge.

Also challenging were a few former members who made it their life mission to take others out of the church with them. These few people were not content to leave quietly. One made it his mission to maintain an email group where he gave regular updates on all the bad things happening at Wilshire in their absence. He appeared to watch the live stream and count how many people were in the choir or in the pews. He celebrated the decline in giving and spewed out all manner of misleading statistics to justify his anger. What I found most frustrating about this subterfuge was that his friends either did not or could not stop him. Why could the many kind people of goodwill who had left us not tell their friend that he was out of line and acting out of anger?

The other tragic reality was seeing a few young adults forced to leave the church not because they personally objected to our stance but because their parents or siblings objected and pressured them.

The most surprising thing that happened well after the vote was the periodic loss of members who were onboard with LGBTQ inclusion but couldn't abide the church's growing social awareness in the age of Trump. Despite conscious efforts by our staff not to be provocative, we as a church have been engaged in the work of racial conciliation, acknowledgment of the #MeToo movement, speaking up against the United States government separating refugee parents from their children at the border, and other issues that are clearly biblically based. Wilshire historically has been a counterbalance to the right-wing voices of a few prominent megachurch pastors in Dallas, but those pastors' solid identification with Donald Trump has shifted the dynamic to make our position suddenly seem more political than ever before. Had our congregation not splintered over the LGBTQ issue at the time of the 2016 presidential election, I wonder if we would have splintered anyway over the current state of affairs in our country.

A study reported in August 2018 by LifeWay Research found 57 percent of Protestant churchgoers under age fifty prefer to go to church with people who share their political views.[1] Increasingly, few adult Protestants say they attend church with people who have differing political views than their own. Given that data and given the way traditionalists heard pro-LGBTQ comments in every sermon and prayer and Bible study for two years at Wilshire, I have to suspect that Trump voters likewise would hear anti-Trump messages in every sermon and prayer and Bible study today. From my perspective, that's because so many of the issues and values promoted by the Trump administration run headlong against the teachings of the Bible in unavoidable ways: welcoming refugees, loving neighbor as self, caring for the least of these, respecting all people created in the image of God.

What we've tried to preserve in our rebuilding years is a sense of middle ground, a place for both progressives and centrists. But just as the theology of same-sex acceptance cannot seem to span the full spectrum in one church, so the politics of liberal all the way to conservative may not be able to span the full spectrum in one church.

The fact that our LGBTQ vote happened on the same week as the 2016 presidential election may have obscured these two separate issues that are no doubt among the most divisive issues facing the modern church.

1. Bob Smietana, "Many Churchgoers Want to Worship with People Who Share Their Politics," LifeWay Research, August 23, 2018, https://tinyurl.com/yarn3nj2.

21. For the Joy Set before You

When our pastor walks babies around the sanctuary for dedication, he always says this important line: "We pray that this child would have a good life, not an easy life." The reason, of course, is that to live a life of meaning is not to live an easy life. A good life is not an easy life.

This is an important lesson for churches and denominational bodies to learn as they consider one of the most challenging questions of our time: how to address the inclusion of persons who are gay, lesbian, transgender, or otherwise nonconforming to traditional roles. Taking up this question is not easy, but it is necessary.

Yet most pastors and churches would rather talk about almost anything but human sexuality, and for good reason: "It's just too hard." "It's too divisive." "I'll get fired." "We'll lose giving." "We'll lose members."

If you've read this far in the book, you've glimpsed the sorrow and the joy of having this conversation. And you're likely just as afraid as you ever were to have this conversation in your church.

Here's the main message I want to convey: The avoidance of conflict that appears to be a good life is actually only a substitute for an illusory easy life. And in this case, easy is not good. In hindsight, we are better for choosing the good over the easy. We are better for having had the conversation.

In Hebrews 12:1–3, we read these words:

> Therefore, since we are surrounded by so great a cloud of witnesses, let us also lay aside every weight and the sin that clings so closely, and let us run with perseverance the race that is set before us, looking to Jesus the pioneer and perfecter of our faith, who for the sake of the joy that was set before him endured the cross, disregarding its shame, and has taken his seat at the right hand of the throne of God.

Consider him who endured such hostility against himself from sinners, so that you may not grow weary or lose heart.

For the sake of the joy that was set before him. We learn from the life of Jesus that we can and must take on difficult tasks for the sake of the joy that will come later.

This has certainly been our experience. The joy we have found in welcoming into church life those who have been rejected and expelled and maligned by the church is beyond measure.

Congregations that open themselves to full participation by those in the LGBTQ community are likely to begin hearing the other side of the story they have missed for so long, and that story includes a lot of hidden pain. Individuals and families who have faced exclusion but want to be part of a community of faith carry emotional and spiritual pain that cannot be simply washed away in a moment. After our vote, we had a visit from a couple who drove thirty miles to get to our church. On the line of our guest card we ask, "Are you a member of another church?" They wrote, "Yes, but we were asked not to come back."

I mourn the loss of most of the folks who left our church over the LGBTQ vote, but I also realize there are a hundred other churches in Dallas where they can land and find community. But for those who are coming to us now, there aren't five other churches in our part of Dallas where they could be restored to faith and know the joy of their salvation. That's a trade-off I would make again and again.

As a pastor or lay leader in a church, why should you take the risk of having a conversation about LGBTQ inclusion? The negative answers are obvious: You could lose your job. You could lose financial support. You could lose your friends. You could be embarrassed publicly. You could be kicked out of some other group. But the positive answers should be equally obvious: You could help more people find faith in Jesus Christ. You could set an example of the love of Jesus. You could become a beacon of hope to other churches. You could gain members and gain finances. You could save someone's life.

Evangelical Christians love to preach and teach on Philippians 2:

> Do nothing from selfish ambition or conceit, but in humility regard others as better than yourselves. Let each of you look not to your own interests, but to the interests of others. Let the same mind be in you that was in Christ Jesus, who, though he was in the form of God, did not regard equality with God as something to be exploited, but emptied himself, taking the form of a slave, being born in human likeness. And being found in human form, he humbled himself and became obedient to the point of death—even death on a cross. Therefore God also highly exalted him and gave him the name that is above every name, so that at the name of Jesus every knee should bend, in heaven and on earth and under the earth, and every tongue should confess that Jesus Christ is Lord, to the glory of God the Father.

Following the example of Jesus does not guarantee your retirement funds, does not ensure keeping your friends, and does not assure you of an invitation to the denominational awards banquet. Following Jesus requires humility to the point of death—maybe not just physical death, by the way, but perhaps death of standing or acclamation in the eyes of others.

I'm not going to say this is easy to do. I and others in our church leadership have physical and spiritual wounds to show for the road we've taken. It is exhausting. It is nerve-racking. It is hard work. But it's also the right thing to do. It's the road to a good life, but not an easy life.

My plea to you is not that you should follow the exact road our congregation has taken. It's not even to beg you to become inclusive of the LGBTQ community. My plea is for you and your church to have the courage to have the conversation, not to hide in fear of hard questions. You may come down in a different place than we have, and that's OK—so long as you know why you believe what you say you believe.

This is a hard conversation. Have the conversation anyway.

Appendix A: Common Questions and Objections

Why didn't Wilshire do a congregational survey?

Our study group made an intentional decision not to conduct a congregational survey on attitudes toward LGBTQ inclusion. The reason was that the group had been asked to study the issue themselves and make recommendations, not to take the temperature of the room and figure out how to keep it comfortable for as many people as possible.

One of the earliest understandings of the study group was that the average person in the pew had not studied this issue deeply and so lacked a framework to understand the various positions put forward. We knew this because it also was true of the members of the study group.

A survey would have been helpful if the goal had been to find out what a majority of the congregation believed and then codify that. But this was neither the mandate nor the desire of the study group.

Why weren't Wilshire's leaders willing to wait and let this work out over a longer period of time?

A senior adult said to one of our study group members, "It is obvious where this issue is moving in America. And so I know that twenty years from now, this will not be an issue at all. But could we please just have our church as it is until we die?" That opinion was shared by more than a few people who just wanted to keep the peace for their own benefit in the latter years of their lives.

The fundamentalist in me wants to quote Joshua 24:15: "Choose this day whom you will serve." Nowhere in the Bible are we taught to wait to follow God until it's easier to do so.

Further, it always feels safe to a majority population to wait a little longer to make room for a minority population. Only when we put ourselves in the place of the other do we understand the sense of urgency.

A corollary to the senior adult's perspective cited above is to say the church should not discuss or act on LGBTQ inclusion because it will create division, and avoiding division is the utmost goal. This viewpoint seems reasonable only to someone who lives within an established place of privilege. Not talking about it will not preclude divisions over it. I was perpetually astounded by traditionalists in the church who feared losing members if we became more inclusive but could not comprehend that we would lose members if we failed to become more inclusive, which was the truth.

For us, this decision in a way boiled down to choosing between keeping the current church comfortable while people died off or welcoming a new generation of the church as we built for the future.

Won't a vote for inclusion damage the church's reputation in the community?

This concern was frequently mentioned by opponents to change in our congregation. In my notes from the various roundtable dialogues, I summarized these expressions: "Concerned about damaging church's reputation as a solid, biblical church, that we would become known as radical rather than a true Bible-teaching church, that new members would mainly be gay or transgender and we would no longer attract young families. Also concerned about public expressions of physical affection that would make it uncomfortable for families to be at Wilshire."

Often, when people talked about damaging our reputation in the community, what they meant was damaging their reputation with their friends who attend other churches. A recurring theme, when honestly spoken, was how they would endure the ridicule of their golf group, bridge group, Friday-night dinner group, or country club friends. And on this point, we likely had failed as church leaders, because we had not provided sufficient information to prepare our members to speak kindly and knowledgeably with their friends.

The answer to this question also depends on what kind of community you find yourself in. For us, situated in conservative North Dallas, with a Bible church or megachurch or Southern Baptist church everywhere you go, we already were an outlier because we ordained women and sang from a hymnal. The test of friendship had been stretched over these issues, but welcoming the LGBTQ community would just be too much.

What we discovered after our vote was that those in the community who already didn't like us still didn't like us, but many who didn't know us before came running to learn about us and to embrace us. Community relations definitely improved rather than deteriorated.

Is this decision anything like accepting divorced persons or singles in leadership?

The vast majority of Christian churches in America today attempt to treat never-married adults the same way as married adults. That is a shift that has happened in my lifetime. Whatever perceived prohibition there was against a single person being a deacon or pastor or committee chair has faded away. And many churches, including ours, no longer hand out scarlet letters to those who have experienced divorce.

Here's the way George Mason addressed this: "Some of us have lived long enough to remember when people got divorced in the church and stopped coming. There was a kind of shunning that took place. And then would the church remarry anyone who was divorced? It appears to be very plain in the Scripture about that.

"Most people forget that at the very same time we decided here at Wilshire whether we would ordain women as deacons, we also asked whether we would ordain a single person who never had been married or a divorced person. No one ever successfully presented a hermeneutical argument that convinced anyone about that issue. What happened was a lot of people in our church, in our families, got divorced, got remarried. We determined we wanted grace to win the day. It changed the way we looked at Scripture."

In fairness, though, it must be noted that people choose to be divorced and often (but not always) choose to be single. We now understand that people do not choose to be gay, lesbian, bisexual, or transgender. That puts the question of LGBTQ inclusion in a different category than marriage or divorce.

Is it fair to compare LGBTQ inclusion to racial inclusion or gender inclusion?

This is a hot topic, because those who favor inclusion often will say, "Discriminating against LGBTQ persons is just like the church's history of excluding black people and women." And in their minds, this is a reasonable comparison. Oppose LGBTQ inclusion today, and you're going to look like your racist ancestors in the lens of history.

On the other side of the equation, traditionalists find this to be comparing apples to oranges. In their view, race and gender are things you have no control over, but many traditionalists still believe sexual orientation is at least partially chosen. Whatever amount of scientific and medical evidence we have today that says sexual orientation is not a choice has not yet convinced them otherwise. And even among those who might concede that sexual orientation isn't a choice, many believe same-sex attraction is a burden that must be held in check, viewing it as a vice or sinful inclination.

And that comparison will set off anger in the LGBTQ community. Consider this often-used statement from well-meaning Christians: "I'm a sinner, too, just like you. It's just that my sin is different from yours." A fundamental breakdown in communication occurs when same-sex attraction is labeled as a "sin," because most people believe sins are things you can choose not to do. Which brings us back to the question of nature versus nurture.

Traditionalists never want to be called "bigots." And yet to progressives, the very act of denying full identity to the LGBTQ community smacks of bigotry.

The Merriam-Webster.com dictionary defines a bigot as "a person who is obstinately or intolerantly devoted to his or her own opinions and prejudices" or especially "one who regards or treats the members of a group (such as a racial or ethnic group) with hatred and intolerance." Where is the line between disagreement and hatred? That line is always brighter for the person who feels hated and always dimmer for the person who is accused of hatred or intolerance.

One thing to the credit of the most fundamentalist churches in America today is that they don't mind being called "bigots" or "haters." They have drawn clear and definite lines that must not be crossed, and whatever that gets them labeled, so be it. The struggle arises for those who try to mark out some ground in the middle.

A member of our study group reported a congregant's concern that they would be forced to make a choice between being pro-gay or anti-gay. Said the study group member: "I've heard no one say in this class that we shouldn't welcome gays into our church; they all believe we should. They feel there is a concern that if they take the more conservative view, they will be labeled as anti-gay."

Is the church bowing to secular culture in accepting same-sex behavior?

Another common argument against full inclusion is that the church is merely bowing to the secular agenda of modern culture. Witness this exchange within our study group:

Traditionalist: "Just because it happened in our culture doesn't mean we need to change what we've been teaching."

Progressive: "If you are a gay Christian, you may say, 'Get over this. Let's talk about something that matters.' There are things Jesus was focused on, and gay marriage was not one of them. Get the little stuff out of the way, and deal with what makes a difference."

Traditionalist: "I would beg to differ because of other verses that talk about how important sexual purity is. We should, as a congregation and community, worry about sexual purity and the problems that come."

No doubt, American culture has become more permissive over time—although Christians seem to be quite selective about when and where they apply judgment on these matters. Most of American Christianity has adapted to changing trends in clothing, music, architecture, hair styles, women in the workforce, alcohol consumption, and a host of other things. Which is to say that the church always is reacting to cultural trends and influences.

The question is how to determine which of those cultural influences are about things that matter and which are about things that do not matter as much. It's not just that the church must choose its battles wisely, but also that some things are essential to the faith, and some things are not. Traditionalists are saying that prohibiting same-sex relations is essential to the faith, and progressives are saying this is not essential. That's the root of the problem.

Thus the frustration of one member of our study group, who in exasperation declared one night, "I thought our goal was to recommend policy for the church, not to decide whether being gay is a sin or whether people are born gay. Are we really trying to come up with consensus on whether it's OK to be gay?"

How did the legalization of same-sex marriage change the dynamic for the church?

For the first time in the history of the church, gay people can get married legally. For two millennia before, the church had made the argument that gay persons must, like straight persons, be celibate as long as they are not married. In the case of a gay person, that meant forever, because marriage was not an option.

Now the church must ask whether it will continue with that line of thinking or will embrace a similar standard for both straight and gay couples. The church no longer can use the legal limits of marriage as an excuse not to talk about the more difficult issues of creation and human sexuality.

Thus, the legalization of same-sex marriage stands as a turning point for the church in America. We cannot act like nothing new has happened. Every church must ask how it will respond to this new reality.

The Baptist General Convention of Texas, the largest state Baptist body in America, noted this decision point in a news release shortly after the court ruling: "We recommend churches adopt bylaws and employment policies that clearly define its religious position regarding marriage and that clearly state how church staff and facilities are to be used in light of those religious beliefs."[1] The state organization drafted suggested guidelines for churches to prevent them from having to perform same-sex weddings, including suggested language for bylaws revisions.

More than anything, the Supreme Court ruling forced the church to come out from behind the easy protection of preaching no sex outside of marriage and to declare its true beliefs on same-sex relationships.

The ancillary consequence of this was a renewed need to discuss heterosexual sexual ethics. Also influenced by changing cultural mores, the church largely didn't want to have a conversation about men and women living together without the benefit of marriage, about premarital sex or teenage sex, or about anything else difficult to discuss.

Why is this suddenly an issue, when for two thousand years, the church didn't talk about it?

A member of the study group asked, "This idea that the Scripture doesn't speak of same-sex relationships seems to be a fairly recent interpretation. Why? Why didn't theologians come up with this three hundred years ago?"

Here's the answer George Mason gave that night in our context: "We are an extremely well-educated group of people. We have access to enormous amounts of information, Bibles, translations, commentaries. There is a sense in which that is pretty new in the history of the world. There have been throughout the ages erudite people, especially from the Reformation on. Prior to that time, the Bible was not accessible to most people.

"In the Reformation, authority gets relocated to the Bible. We have only the last half millennium where there has been attention on the

1. John Litzler, "What the Supreme Court's Same-Sex Marriage Ruling Means for Texas Churches," *txb.life* (blog of Baptist General Convention of Texas), June 26, 2015, https://tinyurl.com/y6u87qqq.

written word of God, interpreted by educated clergy. Especially in the twentieth century, there was a question of how to interpret the Bible.

"There are other examples of how we have rethought things: nineteenth-century slavery, when the church first determined Christians should not treat their slaves in mean ways but kindly. The church said slavery is still valid, but then the Christian conscience came to a breaking point on that, even though the Bible didn't change. The community said we think the living Word is telling the church to no longer sustain the institution of slavery.

"We are in a place like this on this issue, where there has been a growing sense that the church has moved from blanket condemnation of all same-sex behavior and inclination to an often-benign attitude and now to taking another look at it. The Christian church lives with a tension between the living Word and the written word."

Why are clergy often more progressive on this issue than the congregations they serve?

There came a moment late in our study group's work when I was asked a question I knew might require a surprising answer. The question was how many of our ministerial staff members (fourteen at the time) we would lose if the church voted to be fully inclusive of the LGBTQ community.

My answer: None. Then I explained that we as a staff had discussed this from the beginning, with our senior pastor plainly telling staff that this conversation could lead to staff layoffs and budget reductions. And to a person, our staff members said, "Have the conversation anyway." Some of us had come to a more inclusive position recently, and others had held a more inclusive view as long as they could remember. It turned out we all had arrived at the same destination but via different routes and schedules.

This was understandably shocking news to the traditionalists in the study group. "Do you mean there's not a single minister on our staff who holds my view?" one member asked. "Yes," I replied, adding that we had not gone out and systematically hired all affirming clergy; in reality, most of our staff are so long-tenured and were hired so long ago that such questions wouldn't have been asked. Again, we all got to the same destination via different routes.

Why is this so? The starting point is to realize that most educated clergy have spent more time studying and thinking about Scripture and sexuality than the typical layperson. If nothing else, that study and a life experience in ministry will lead most clergy to acknowledge they have more questions than answers. Well-trained clergy also know the dangers of stretching biblical interpretation and certainty too far.

Nevertheless, educated clergy often are treated with suspicion on such matters, as though education has ruined them. This is perhaps unique to matters religious, where education may be seen as a threat rather than a help.

Compare the work of clergy to the work of medical doctors. Let's say you have a brain tumor, and you go to visit your doctor for evaluation and treatment. Would you be reassured if your doctor said, "I know there are new treatments and schools of thought on this, but I prefer to rely on what I first learned in medical school in 1954"?

You would be horrified. Yet when it comes to clergy, parishioners often want their pastors not to have been influenced by recent scholarship or commentary that sheds new light on Scripture. Such new information is inherently viewed as liberal or suspect. But why should we want our doctors to be better educated than our clergy?

Even when clergy have studied and are willing to admit changing their views on issues like same-sex attraction, their voices are discounted. Imagine again you're seeing a doctor to treat a brain tumor. You take a friend with you to the appointment. After the doctor explains the current best treatment plan, based upon her extensive medical education and experience, your friend chimes in: "Well, I've read on the Internet about an old-fashioned treatment that doesn't require the pain of surgery or the risk of infection. You should follow this plan instead." Would you listen to the doctor or to the friend?

In churches across America, Christians pondering theological issues time after time choose the Internet-educated friend over the seminary-educated pastor because the friend's counsel is less threatening and requires less adaptation.

This is not to say that all well-educated clergy will come down on the side of full LGBTQ inclusion in the church. Remember, Christians of good faith may interpret the Scriptures differently on this issue—and they do.

What I can say with certainty is that there are far more pastors in America today who at least have doubts about the traditional interpretation of the so-called clobber verses against same-sex relations than pastors who are able to stand in the pulpit and admit those doubts.

Is it possible to keep traditionalists and progressives together in the same church while addressing this issue?

During our study group debates, one member asked about LGBTQ inclusion, "Why is this such a hot issue? We're not debating the resurrection." To which another member replied, "I want my child taught the way I believe." And the original questioner responded, "But we have others who believe the same thing on the other side; they want their kids to be taught that it's OK if they are gay. Is there a way for us to be church together?"

This is a much harder reality than any of us would like to admit. Progressives are, by definition, more tolerant of dissent and more comfortable living amid differing views. Conservatives, or traditionalists in this case, are by definition more concerned about "conserving" a point of view and therefore less tolerant of keeping fellowship with those who disagree with them. While progressives may believe they are advocating on behalf of the marginalized or excluded, conservatives may counter that they, too, are being marginalized or excluded.

One of the most conservative members of our study group lamented after the congregational roundtables, "It was very difficult to sit and have the opinion I have and hear people say the reasons they have. For people [like me] to be comfortable, it is going to be difficult."

Throughout our study, we noted that those who favor full inclusion had for years bided their time and continued to joyfully participate in the church, even though they thought we were too restrictive. Those same people assumed (wrongly, it turns out) that if the tide turned on church practice and opinion, their more conservative friends would likewise bide their time and continue to joyfully participate in the church. But such was not to be.

The best framework I've encountered to explain the inherent differences between conservatives and liberals—a framework that is not perfect yet is informative—is offered by George Lakoff, cognitive scientist at the University of California, Berkeley. In *Moral Politics*, he explains two perspectives that shape two different definitions of what is "moral":

Conservatives most often embrace a Strict Father model of life, which begins with the idea that "life is difficult and that the world is fundamentally dangerous."[2] As in a "traditional" nuclear family, a strong father figure must dominate, authority must be preserved at all costs, and children must learn lessons through hard knocks and punishment. The Strict Father model values "discipline, authority, order, boundaries, homogeneity, purity and self-interest."[3]

Liberals most often embrace a Nurturing Parent model of life, which begins with the idea that proper nurture within a loving family unit will lead children to become nurturing adults who care for themselves and others. This model values "empathy, nurturance, self-nurturance, social ties, fairness and happiness."[4]

These political identities spill over into religious identities, Lakoff says. In conservative forms of religion, God is a Strict Father who, in effect, says, "Do as I say, and you will get to Heaven; otherwise, you will burn in hell—punished painfully forever!" Who decides what God meant? A conservative Christian pastor is given that authority

---

2. George Lakoff, *Moral Politics*, 3rd ed. (Chicago: University of Chicago Press, 2016), 65.
3. Lakoff, *Moral Politics*, 110.
4. Lakoff, *Moral Politics*, 113.

by his church. In progressive forms of religion, God is a Nurturant Parent who offers grace, love, forgiveness and fulfillment."[5]

Progressives, or liberals, labor under the impression that if they can just present enough facts, they will reason with their conservative friends and help them see the light. Yet the very nature of brain science says this is not likely to happen, short of a near-cataclysmic event in a person's life. "And so year after year, decade after decade, liberals keep telling facts to conservative audiences without changing many minds," Lakoff says. "This behavior by liberals is itself a form of science denial—the denial of the cognitive and brain sciences."[6]

I am increasingly convinced there's only a certain distance that can be spanned in any single religious body, whether local church or denomination. Think of the four views on same-sex relations outlined in chapter 16, ranging from Viewpoint A to Viewpoint D. The previous pattern in the church was to span from Viewpoint A to Viewpoint B, from strictly condemning all same-sex thought as evil to condemning only same-sex activity as evil. Compared with Viewpoint A, the Viewpoint B folks considered themselves quite progressive. And in reality, these two views were close enough at root to allow conversation.

Think of this like holding a rubber band with a fixed limit. That band could stretch from the A position to the B position and not break. But it cannot stretch from the A position to the C position without rupture. When Viewpoint C enters the picture and a congregation agrees to try to accommodate the next level of inclusion, the bracket of the rubber band shifts to the left and leaves the Viewpoint A folks out entirely; it's a bridge too far. The question becomes whether a church can truly span from Viewpoint B to Viewpoint C without rupture (or from Viewpoint C to D), and the experience of churches across America says this, too, is often not possible.

5. Lakoff, Moral Politics, 432.
6. Lakoff, Moral Politics, 267

How can an inclusive congregation teach children and youth about sexuality without making it all about same-sex relations?

George Mason addressed this question in a pastoral letter he wrote to our congregation along with the report of the study group. Here's what he said:

> It will not be our goal to make kids want to "turn" gay, because that is simply not the way it works. Nor would it be our desire to advocate sexual promiscuity of any kind, gay or straight. We want to teach about faithful covenantal relationships.
>
> Within the youth group, Darren [our youth minister] already teaches about developing a healthy, Christian sexual ethic that can be summarized as chastity before marriage and faithfulness in it. This ethic is built on the three pillars of mutuality, equality, and commitment. This ethic is equally applicable to both same-sex and opposite-sex relationships, even though Darren at present does not speak of same-sex relationships. It would be easy to apply the same standards expected of opposite-sex relationships to same-sex relationships. So, Darren would not need to radically change the message being taught to youth.
>
> With youth, we currently stress and would continue to stress the benefits of waiting to enter sexual relationships more than the potential dangers. Our intention has been to approach conversations about sex from a positive position that is tied to Christian discipleship. Unfortunately, Christians have sometimes portrayed sex as something dirty that is to be avoided until suddenly it becomes clean immediately after marriage. This is inevitably confusing and leads to experiences of shame when sexual discipline is not observed, instead of the healthier sense of guilt that can be forgiven. We never have wanted to try to scare kids away from sex, because that approach simply doesn't work. At the same time, we want them to understand the desire of God

for us to enjoy sexual relations within covenantal relationships as a human reflection of fully committed divine intimacy.

Appendix B: Q&A about the Study Group

The following question-and-answer document was distributed to the church when the study group was named and announced.

Why are we doing this?

- The Deacon Nominating Committee has made a request to the deacon officers for guidance in its work, specifically asking to know if a member's sexual orientation should be a consideration in eligibility for deacon service.
- In addition, the senior pastor has asked for guidance on how the church should respond to the recent Supreme Court ruling legalizing same-sex marriage, believing this needs to be a deliberate and open decision process of the church. These two things, although separate in origin, have combined at this moment in time to require special study by the congregation, beginning with the deacons.
- Currently, there is no language in Wilshire's bylaws to provide any instruction—either pro or con—on these issues.
- Concurrently, questions have been asked about what is meant by the emphasis on "inclusion" and "diversity" that ranked at the top of the Vision 20/20 member-input process. It seems that while we as a congregation highly valued these concepts, we do not all mean the same thing when we use the same words. The present moment seems like an appropriate time to answer this question.

But isn't the Bible absolutely clear on this?

- Christians of goodwill read and interpret the Bible differently regarding same-sex relations. One of the first tasks of the study group will be to wrestle with the theological contexts and interpretations relevant to this conversation.

- There are seven biblical texts that are most often associated with discussions regarding homosexuality. The study group will wrestle with each of these plus the larger witness of Scripture.
- It is Wilshire's history to study, pray, and listen for the direction of the Holy Spirit.

Is this just a reaction to the Supreme Court ruling on same-sex marriage?

- No, this has been a matter of conversation among church leadership prior to the Supreme Court ruling this summer.
- The Deacon Nominating Committee has wrestled with this issue for several years, and for several years the senior pastor has asked the committee not to ask for changes to current practices, believing the time was not right for such a conversation.
- Wilshire's bylaws currently contain no language indicating openness or limitations on same-sex marriages, who may be ordained, who may have a family dedication, etc. The study group may choose to recommend limitations just as well as it may choose to recommend openness.

Doesn't asking questions about this put Wilshire on the liberal side of things already?

- No, asking questions and seeking to learn more about Scripture and God's work in the world today is neither a conservative nor a liberal agenda.
- It is the Wilshire Way to study, pray, learn, follow process, and make informed decisions.
- Other congregations like Wilshire are finding their own ways to study the same issues today.

Has an outcome already been determined?

- No. The study group has full authorization to chart its own course and has been given no preferred outcome to achieve.
- There is a full range of possibilities that might emerge from this study, perhaps creating more openness in some areas and yet limitations in others. This is not merely an all-in or all-out proposition.

What is the timeline?

- The study group will be given all the time it needs to thoroughly research the issues, pray, and seek divine guidance. Ideally, a report will emerge by spring 2016 or fall 2016 at the latest, but these are not hard-and-fast deadlines.

How was the study group named?

- In keeping with Wilshire's practice on previous issues that required extensive study, the deacon officers sought to appoint a study group that represents the diversity of the congregation in age, gender, theological perspective, and length of membership.
- The study group includes long-time members, newer members, older and younger adults, married and single adults, and one youth representative.

How may I give input to the study group?

- Comments or suggestions may be addressed to the study group's chairman or to any member of the group.
- Whether the study group will seek additional congregational input will be determined by the group when it convenes.

What will be done with the study group's findings?

- Whatever the study group comes up with will be brought first to the deacon body for consideration.
- The deacons then will determine whether anything requires consideration or action by the church at large.
- If any changes are proposed to the church bylaws or policies, those changes would be brought by the deacons to the church in conference and to any committees affected by the changes.

Appendix C: What the Bible Says about Same-Sex Relationships

Within the Old Testament, there are four passages most frequently cited as giving direct reference to same-sex relationships. The first two are remarkably similar, although appearing in different books and happening at different times to different people. It is likely that you may have read or heard only the first of these near-parallel accounts, which is the story of Sodom. It is found in Genesis 19:1–11.

The gist of the story is that Lot, Abraham's relative, was living in Sodom when two "angels" came to visit him. He begged them to spend the night in the safety of his house, and upon nightfall, "the men of Sodom, both young and old, all the people to the last man, surrounded the house" and demanded that Lot turn over his house-guests for their sexual appetites. Lot offered the men his two virgin daughters instead, but that wouldn't do, and Lot barely escaped harm himself.

A similar story is told in Judges 19:16–30 but is located in the village of Gibeah. This story is gorier than the Genesis story, because the guest's concubine is "wantonly raped" and "abused . . . all through the night until the morning." The guest then takes his concubine home on a donkey, only to cut her into twelve pieces, limb by limb, and send her parts throughout all the territory of Israel as a warning.

Biblical scholarship would demand that we ask why there are two such similar stories told in different places and from different times within the Bible. But that is a journey we do not have time to take today. So let's focus for the moment on the Genesis story, because this is where we get the word *sodomy*, a synonym for homosexual and other kinds of taboo sexual acts, particularly oral and anal sex.

The concept of sexuality in the Old Testament presents challenges to modern-day Christians because of the patriarchal culture, the commonness of men taking multiple wives and keeping concubines. Reading texts such as these requires thoughtful consideration of cultural norms across time.

Many who have held a "traditional" interpretation of the Bible see the story of Sodom as being about homosexuality: the men of Sodom are wicked because they want to have male-on-male sex with the visiting angels. This was true of the translators of the King James Bible, who applied the word "sodomites" to certain New Testament passages, which we'll hear more about in a moment.

Other modern interpreters—including many conservative evangelicals who believe the Bible condemns homosexuality—read the sin of Sodom as being something other than homosexuality. These stories recorded in Genesis and Judges are viewed by them as more about hospitality and justice than about homosexuality as a sexual lifestyle. The larger part of both stories, according to this view, is the need for hosts to protect their guests, which aligns with what we know of ancient Middle Eastern concepts of hospitality.

We are challenged to read these texts from the standpoint of the male-dominant culture of the time, in which femininity was perceived as weakness. Thus, for a male to be put in the position of a female was to be demeaned in the most extreme manner. And for another clue to interpretation, look to Ezekiel 16:49, which refers to the sin of Sodom not as one of sexual immorality but rather of justice: "This was the guilt of your sister Sodom: she and her daughters had pride, excess of food, and prosperous ease, but did not aid the poor and needy."[1]

So to summarize, there are at least three ways to look at the Genesis and Judges passages: (1) They mean what the traditional inter-

---

1. We also find references to Sodom in Isa 10:1–17; Isa 3:9; Jer 23:14; Ezek 16:49; and Zeph 2:8–11. In these passages, Sodom is singled out as a model for greed, injustice, inhospitality, abuse of wealth, abuse of the poor, and general wickedness. Jesus also references Sodom and Gomorrah in Matt 10:14–15, where he says those who reject the welcome of his disciples will be "worse than" Sodom and Gomorrah, an apparent reference to arrogance and lack of hospitality.

pretation has been, that the men of Sodom (and Gibeah) are given as examples to us of the evil of same-sex relations. (2) These passages are not about gays and lesbians but rather hospitality, but that doesn't take away from other, clearer condemnations of same-sex relations later in the Bible. (3) These passages are not about loving same-sex relationships but rather hospitality, and that is part of a larger translation or interpretation problem within the Bible.

The next two Old Testament passages are found in Leviticus. This is the book that is chock-full of rules and regulations for the Hebrew people. The two passages in question are single sentences each. Leviticus 18:22 says, "You shall not lie with a male as with a woman; it is an abomination." Leviticus 20:13 says, "If a man lies with a male as with a woman, both of them have committed an abomination; they shall be put to death; their blood is upon them."

The traditional and widespread reading of these passages is that they are explicitly clear and mean exactly what they say. There is no room or need for further interpretation. And no doubt, that has been the majority view throughout Christian history—although modern Christians have not advocated the death penalty in such cases. And yet, biblical scholars today are split in their interpretations, with even some conservative scholars arguing that the face-value reading is not the best reading.

Both Leviticus passages are part of the Old Testament Holiness Code, which extends from chapters 17 through 26. This code for living was given to separate the children of Israel from their pagan neighbors. It contains hundreds of rules.

One common theme of the Holiness Code was the requirement to keep things separate. For example, fields could not be sown with two kinds of seed, and garments could not be made of two different materials (see Lev 19:19). This theme was intended to demonstrate the need for separation from the surrounding culture. The children of Israel were to live out a vivid picture of what it meant to be separated out as God's people.

There are at least two ways to understand the Holiness Code in a modern Christian context. One is that prohibitions against idolatry and sexual immorality are carried over into the New Testament view, while other prohibitions no longer apply to the Christian community. A second view would agree that prohibitions against idolatry and sexual immorality are carried over into the New Testament era but would disagree about what constitutes sexual immorality based only on an understanding of sexual orientation.

Also, some will suggest that male gender superiority continues to be a factor in this context. Read carefully the laws of Leviticus, and notice where the death penalty is prescribed for odd things that all tie in to maintaining the superior role of adult males: children who curse parents, adultery as the unlawful use of a man's property, and so on. Some modern scholars therefore read the Levitical admonitions against a man lying with a man "as with a woman" as being concerned with making one of the men ritually unclean by penetration. The word *toevah*, translated as "abomination," may refer to becoming ritually unclean, the same as a man lying with a woman during her menstruation, which is forbidden.

To summarize: For Christians of both the views I've just outlined, the hardest part of the Leviticus passages is understanding the Holiness Code in a Christian context. There are many aspects of the Levitical code that even the most conservative Christians would not see as binding on them today. But there are other parts of this Levitical code that a majority of modern Christians might easily believe still to be relevant today. How are we to know the difference?

For Christians, the New Testament holds greater authority than the Old Testament, so we turn now to see what the New Testament might teach us.

Like me, you may have grown up carrying a "red-letter" edition of the Bible. These special Bibles show every word attributed to Jesus in red type for emphasis. And that makes sense on several levels, because historic Christianity has placed a higher value on what Jesus said and taught than on what others, even the apostle Paul, wrote or taught. So, turning to the New Testament, we might first ask, "What did Jesus say about homosexuality?" In the strictest sense, Jesus said absolutely nothing about homosexuality. We cannot turn to a red-letter verse that either approves or disapproves of same-sex relationships in the way we might hope.

Instead, the three most frequently cited New Testament passages mentioning homosexuality all are attributed to Paul. Let's look first at 1 Corinthians 6:9–11 and 1 Timothy 1:9–11.

The 1 Corinthians passage says, "Do you not know that wrongdoers will not inherit the kingdom of God? Do not be deceived! Fornicators, idolaters, adulterers, male prostitutes [*malakos* in Greek], sodomites [*arsenokoitai* in Greek], thieves, the greedy, drunkards, revilers, robbers—none of these will inherit the kingdom of God. And this is what some of you used to be. But you were washed, you were sanctified, you were justified in the name of the Lord Jesus Christ and in the Spirit of our God."

The 1 Timothy passage says, "This means understanding that the law is laid down not for the innocent but for the lawless and disobedient, for the godless and sinful, for the unholy and profane, for those who kill their father or mother, for murderers, fornicators, sodomites [*arsenokoitais* in Greek], slave traders, liars, perjurers, and whatever else is contrary to the sound teaching that conforms to the glorious gospel of the blessed God, which he entrusted to me."

In the traditional view, sex between people of the same gender falls clearly within a set of behaviors that are not indicative of those who will inherit the kingdom of God. Same-sex behavior is viewed as similar to other things that are sinful but for which repentance and forgiveness may be sought.

A different view is that everything in the New Testament that condemns same-sex behavior in New Testament times continues to apply to Christian same-sex behavior today. In this view, New Testament condemnations of same-sex behavior include pederasty, male prostitution, and excessive lust that is contrary to one's created nature—not the expression of same-sex affection by those with such an orientation.

These differences of opinion are illustrated in disagreement about the words used in the original Greek here. Paul uses the Greek word *arsenokoitai* here for the first time found in Greek or Jewish literature, so there is no context from which to draw an easy comparison. It appears to be a compound word drawing together "man" and "lying with or sleeping with." From this put-together Greek word, various English translations have embellished with different emphases: "abusers of themselves with mankind" (KJV); "sexual perverts" (RSV); "sodomites" (NKJV, NAB, NRSV); "who are guilty of homosexual perversion" (CEV); "practicing homosexuals" (NAB, 1st ed.).

The word *sodomites* in English was introduced in the King James Bible in 1611. It is found in neither the Hebrew nor the Greek editions of the text. And on a similar note, the word *homosexual* was not used in English literature until the nineteenth century and did not appear in an English translation of the Bible until the midtwentieth century. Taken together, these facts lead adherents of one viewpoint to suggest that Paul actually was talking about the known ancient practices of cultic prostitution or male pederasty (an adult male having sex with a younger boy) or about temple prostitutes, a common issue in his time. Traditional biblical scholars, however, see *arsenokoitai* as Paul's allusion to the Levitical code, meaning a clear reference to same-sex relations. Do not get hung up on the word *sodomites*, they argue, but instead understand that the intent is to describe same-sex relations by any name.

The second word in question, *malakos*, is easier to translate and means "soft," often used to refer to effeminacy. According to a traditional view, this remains a fitting description especially of a male who engages in sexual acts with another male. Other interpreters note that there was another commonly used word that Paul could have chosen here for pederastic relationships. That word is *paiderasste*. They also point out that elsewhere in the New Testament, *malakos* is translated as "soft" or "fine" in reference to clothing (see Matt 11:8 and Luke 7:25). So was Paul referring to "male prostitutes," as the NRSV suggests? Or was he referring to someone lacking virility or manliness? There are several ways to translate this, all in keeping with the primary literal translation, "soft."

To quickly review before we move on: Christians of goodwill and sincere faith come to different conclusions about these Pauline passages, with the argument largely hinging on interpretation of two key words, *arsenokoitai* and *malakos*. The weight of history falls on the side of reading these passages as specifically condemning same-sex relations, but modern scholarship increasingly questions that reading. So here is a case where we have to read and pray and seek divine discernment.

And that brings us now to Romans 1:26–27, which is the single most challenging text to address for those who desire a more progressive view. Even some scholars who dismiss every other biblical text as not relevant to the modern debate over homosexuality see this text as prohibitive. It says, "For this reason God gave them up to degrading passions. Their women exchanged natural intercourse for unnatural, and in the same way also the men, giving up natural intercourse with women, were consumed with passion for one another. Men committed shameless acts with men and received in their own persons the due penalty for their error."

Christians traditionally have interpreted this passage as explicitly prohibitive of same-sex relations, and we can see why. We do not have the same difficulty interpreting here the words "intercourse" or "women" or "men." These are clear in their translations.

What gets contested is the larger point Paul is making in Romans. Some biblical scholars see Paul here linking sexual immorality to idolatry. By this account, the "degrading passions" listed are the result of idolatry. Some traditionalists would agree, to a point, but quickly note that from their view, same-sex behavior is itself a form of idolatry.

Additionally, Paul makes an argument based on the natural order of creation. There are different views on what he means by this. For example, elsewhere Paul uses a similar appeal to nature to justify his position on the proper length of men's and women's hair and the need for women to wear head coverings (1 Cor 11:2–16). That leads some to ask why Christians want to enforce one of the prohibitions but not the others. As with the Old Testament laws, however, traditionalists counter that some of the prohibitions are cultural and others are not. The sexual prohibitions, again, are of a more serious nature.

Advocates of a nontraditional view also note that arguing from nature was a common rhetorical device in Paul's day. It would be similar today to saying, "The conventional wisdom is . . . ." The words in Greek are *physis*, meaning "nature," and *para physin*, meaning "against nature." Look to Romans 11:13–24 for further understanding of these words. There, Paul says God acted "contrary to nature" by grafting gentiles into the tree of God's people, the Jews. Thus, the reading of "against nature" may mean "unconventional" in both cases. The question is whether, since God has shown adaptability, we also should be adaptable in our understanding of what has been considered "conventional."

Another quick recap before we move on: For those with a progressive view, the Romans 1 passage is by far the most challenging of all the biblical passages to address. There are biblical scholars who dismiss every other text as not prohibitive of loving same-sex commitments as we might know them today yet cannot get around the Romans passage. The counterpoint is to say that "contrary to nature" does not mean "unnatural" but rather "unconventional" or even "against the nature of the way a person was made by God."

Apart from the seven biblical passages that are most often cited as direct references to homosexuality, there are other passages that get cited as indirectly condemning same-sex relations, often drawn from the context of marriage. At least one of these does fall in the "red-letter" portion of the New Testament, as recorded in Matthew 19:3–9, which tells the story of the Pharisees coming to test Jesus by asking, "Is it lawful for a man to divorce his wife for any cause?" To which Jesus answers by quoting from Genesis: "Have you not read that the one who made them at the beginning 'made them male and female,' and said, 'For this reason a man shall leave his father and mother and be joined to his wife, and the two shall become one flesh'?"

We find a similar appeal by Paul in Ephesians 5:21–33, a long discourse on wives and husbands being subject to one another and to the Lord. At the end of this, Paul quotes Genesis: "'For this reason a man will leave his father and mother and be joined to his wife, and the two will become one flesh.' This is a great mystery, and I am applying it to Christ and the church. Each of you, however, should love his wife as himself, and a wife should respect her husband."

From a traditional point of view, Jesus's reference to the creation story and appeal to being made "male and female" is a clear statement identifying marriage as exclusively between male and female. Those who adopt this viewpoint find this male-female duality threaded throughout the Bible and therefore indicative of the way God intended creation to function. For this viewpoint, the "one flesh" language becomes extremely important in defining Christian marriage and more.

An alternate reading sees the "one flesh" reference teaching us that their complementarity is first their likeness as human partners, as compared with the prior creation of the animals. This complementarity may include anatomical differences but is fundamentally about being different persons rather than different genders.

Once again, to summarize this section: In a traditional view of creation and marriage, the "one flesh" language of Genesis 2 is important because of the complementary nature of male and female anatomy that is a sign and symbol to us of God's good plan for creation and means for procreation. From another view, "one flesh" also refers to Adam and Eve being created as human companions for each other, apart from the animals, who were not suitable companions for them, and not just to male-female companionship.

Appendix D: The Baptist Pastor and His Transgender Friends

This appendix contains two blog posts I wrote for the opinion page of the Baptist News Global website (https://baptistnews.com). The first post, "Seven Things I'm Learning about Transgender Persons," was published on May 13, 2016. The second post, "Painful Lessons from a Pastor's Viral Transgender Post," appeared on May 31, 2016. Both posts © Baptist News Global. Used by permission.

Seven Things I'm Learning about Transgender Persons

I don't know much about transgender issues, but I'm trying to learn.

How about you? How much do you really know about this subject beyond all the screaming headlines and concerns about who goes to the bathroom where?

The truth is that I don't know any transgender persons—at least I don't think I do. But with the help of a pediatrician friend and a geneticist friend, I'm listening and trying to learn. This is hard, though, because understanding the transgender experience seems so far outside what I have ever contemplated before. And the more I learn, the more theological questions I face as well. This is hard, even for a pastor.

Here's some of what I'm learning from my friends who have experience as medical professionals dealing with real people and real families:

1. Even though LGBT gets lumped together in one tagline, the T is quite different than the LG and B. "Lesbian," "gay" and "bisexual" describe sexual orientation. "Transgender" describes gender identity. These are not the same thing. Sexual orientation is about whom we feel an attraction to and want to mate with; gender identity is about whether we identify as male or female.

2. What you see is not always what you get. For the vast majority of humanity, the presence of male or female genitalia corresponds to whether a person is male or female. What you see is what you are. But for a small part of humanity (something less than 1 percent), the visible parts and the inner identity do not line up. For example, it is possible to be born with male genitalia but female chromosomes or vice versa. And now brain research has demonstrated that it also is possible to be born with female genitalia, female chromosomes but a male brain. Most of us hit the jackpot upon birth with all three factors lining up like cherries on a slot machine: Our anatomy, chromosomes, and brain cells all correspond as either male or female. But some people are born with variations in one or two of these indicators.

3. Stuff happens at birth that most of us never know. It's not an everyday occurrence but it's also not infrequent that babies are born with ambiguous or incomplete sexual anatomy. In the past, surgeons often made the decision about whether this child would be a boy or a girl, based on what was the easiest surgical fix. Today, much more thought is given to these life-changing decisions.

4. Transgender persons are not "transvestites." Far too many of us make this mix-up, in part because the words sound similar and we have no real knowledge of either. Cross-dressers, identified in slang as "transvestites," are people (typically men) who are happy with their gender but derive pleasure from occasionally dressing like the opposite gender. Cross-dressing is about something other than gender identity.

5. Transgender persons are not pedophiles. The typical profile of a pedophile is an adult male who identifies as heterosexual and

most likely even is married. There is zero statistical evidence to link transgender persons to pedophilia.

6. Transgender persons hate all the attention they're getting. The typical transgender person wants desperately not to attract attention. All this publicity and talk of bathroom habits is highly disconcerting to people who have spent their lives trying not to stand out or become the center of attention.

7. Transgender persons are the product of nature much more than nurture. Debate the origins of homosexuality if you'd like and what role nature vs. nurture plays. But for those who are transgender, nature undeniably plays a primary role. According to medical science, chromosomal variances occur within moments of conception, and anatomical development happens within the nine months in the womb. There is no nature vs. nurture argument, except in cases of brain development, which is an emerging field of study.

This last point in particular raises the largest of theological questions. If Christians really believe every person is created in the image of God, how can we damn a baby who comes from the womb with gender dysphoria? My pediatrician friend puts it this way: "We must believe that even if some people got a lower dose of a chromosome, or an enzyme, or a hormonal effect, that does not mean that they got a lower dose of God's image."

I don't know much about transgender issues, but I'm trying to learn—in part because I want to understand the way God has made us. For me, this is a theological quest as much as a biological inquiry or a political cause. How about you?

Painful Lessons from a Pastor's Viral Transgender Post

"Does God still love me?"

That is one of the most painful questions I have been asked in the past two weeks after writing a commentary that went viral and made me a most unlikely spokesperson for the transgender community and their families. As a result of that post being read by more than one million people either online or in print, I have heard the personal stories of people from all over the country. In two weeks' time, I have exchanged personal correspondence with more than 400 people.

Surprisingly, the vast majority of those conversations have been positive—and not just positive but filled with emotion and gratitude—and a fair amount of pain. I have heard from transgender persons, from the parents and friends of transgender persons, from clergy, doctors, teachers, counselors, and lots of average people.

One transgender woman wrote to tell me her story and signed off with these words: "Sincerely, a woman who hopes that God still loves her."

Most transgender persons are not against God; many just fear that God is against them. Or, more specifically, they believe the church is against them. Many of them—a vast number in fact—have grown up in the church and are people of deep faith. But they are people who have been asked not to come back, have been removed from membership, have been shunned. And so have their families.

One of the most heartbreaking messages I received was from a single mom with four kids, including one who is transgender. This entire family recently was kicked out of their church. The mom—who had been accused of child abuse by her pastor for letting her boy dress as a girl—wrote me to ask for help in finding another church in her city where they would be accepted.

Another new friend, as a youth, had been a deeply devoted Bible study leader in his church but was asked not to attend that church anymore after coming out with a non-conforming gender struggle.

And so it is no wonder that people who shared my post on social media often said something like this: "I can't believe I'm sharing something written by a Baptist pastor, but you've got to read this." Sadly, the church of Jesus Christ is most known today for what we're against rather than who God is for.

The following excerpt from an email represents a common sentiment: "You are a pastor from the most conservative, Bible-thumping part of the country. Your quiet words go a long way to helping those who have had no voice. . . . I cry when writing this because of what you are doing and how much it helps and means the world to me."

As the original post indicated, I set out to learn more about transgender persons, to get beyond the headlines and to plunge into something deeper than the toilet wars. And it turns out that in some ways corporate America is doing a better job of addressing the essence of a person's whole self than the church. This is not to say that all of American business has this figured out, but many corporations are trying to learn, trying to do the right thing for their employees. One of the key phrases being used—there even was a TEDx Talk about it—is this: "Bring your whole self to work." The idea is that employees perform better if they don't have to live in fear at work.

Why is corporate America ahead of the church on this? It seems to me Jesus would say, "Bring your whole self to church."

Embracing that idea, though, would require churchgoing folks to be honest in ways that transcend far more than transgender persons. In polite church culture, we have been conditioned to understand that it is dangerous to be our true selves at church—especially if we don't fit the image of a perfect Christian. We say, "Come as you are," but we really mean, "Come as *we* are."

In fact, few among us probably feel free to bring our whole selves to church. We all are fearful of talking about the ways our children have deviated from the norm, our struggles with depression, or financial insecurity, or even food insecurity. One of the other things

I've learned through the years as a pastor is that most church members wait until they're facing foreclosure before asking for help with keeping a house due to unforeseen financial disasters. Most of us only feel like we can talk about the happy stuff, the easy, fluffy stuff, when we come to church.

And in all these conversations of the past two weeks, I have found myself weeping and shaken. I have learned more than I ever imagined—not only about the details of transgender life but also about what it means to be human.

As my commentary went viral, I discovered that the transgender community was immediately kinder to me than the church has been to them. In the commentary, I confessed that I didn't know any transgender persons, or at least I didn't think I did. Immediately upon publication, I began hearing from folks who said this: "I will be your transgender friend." Tears came to my own eyes as I read these lines over and again and realized that I was hearing from strangers who were willing to open their lives to me in much greater proportion than they feared the church would be willing to open itself to them. This is painful and convicting.

One of my new transgender friends told me about attending a church in a very conservative Texas college town and hearing for the first time that God loves him specifically. In this church, the pastor made a point to say not just that God loves everyone but that God loves you, whether you're young or old, male or female, gay or straight, Republican or Democrat, Aggie or Longhorn. And to my new friend, sitting on the back pew of that church, these words sparked a journey back to the faith that had been recently lost.

As a pastor, I'm pretty sure of this one thing: The story of Jesus is much more about who's included rather than who is excluded. "For God so loved the world" includes everyone.

So as my fifteen minutes of fame in the national spotlight fades, here's the most important thing I want to say about all this: God loves you, whoever you are, wherever you are. Whether you're a conservative or a liberal, a traditionalist or a progressive, a Protestant or a Catholic, a male or a female, gay, straight, trans, whatever. God loves you. Now, what are you going to do with that love?

Appendix E: Genetics and Sexuality

The following chapter was written by Gail Brookshire, a member of our congregation and a member of the Inclusion and Diversity Study Group. This is a slightly edited version of a paper she presented to the congregation in 2016 during our study process and is included here with her permission. Gail earned a master of science degree in medical genetics and counseling from the Sarah Lawrence College Human Genetics program. She is board certified by the American Board of Medical Genetics and the American Board of Genetic Counseling. She has thirty-two years of experience as a genetic counselor in the Pediatric Genetics and Metabolism Division at Children's Medical Center of Dallas. She has been a member of the Children's Medical Center Ethics Committee for seventeen years.

Throughout history, people have shown an interest in the vast variety among humankind and nature as a whole. I've always wondered why someone would have bothered to record in Genesis that Esau came out of the womb "red and hairy." I assume that must have been unusual enough to be noteworthy. Centuries went by, and the Augustinian monk Gregor Mendel started taking notes on his pea plants, leading in 1953 to Watson and Crick's unraveling of the structure of DNA: the genetic code behind this beautiful variety observed in mankind and throughout nature.

Since our curiosity about what make us "us" continues, it was to be expected that questions would arise about why some people are attracted to members of their own sex while the majority are attracted to the opposite sex, or why some people experience differences in gender identity. There remain many unanswered questions as to why this would be so, but research has indicated it is likely a combination of genetic, hormonal, and other factors. Many think that nature and nurture both play complex roles; most people experience little or no sense of choice about their sexual orientation.

Gay men are the most studied subset of people who identify as LGB or T, primarily because they tend to identify more clearly as distinctly gay or distinctly straight, as compared to women, whose sexual orientation and identity tend to be more fluid, and are more common than transgender people.[1] Studies estimate that approximately 3.5 to 4 percent of people identify as lesbian, gay, or bisexual and 0.6 percent as transgender.[2] So there are approximately nine million Americans under the umbrella of the LGBT description.

Like many aspects of human behavior, there are probably several underlying causes for gender differences. There are multiple influences that are weighted differently in different people, and these influences contribute to a wide range of outcomes, given the diversity among this population of individuals.

As with most studies related to genetics, the analysis started by looking at families. When large numbers of families were grouped together, it became clear early on that a person who is lesbian or gay is more likely to have family members who are also lesbian or gay as compared to the general population.[3]

Interest spread to studies of siblings, including identical and fraternal twins, as well as singleton siblings. Over the years, twin studies have shown varying concordance rates (meaning both twins are gay or lesbian). A large broad-based study in 2000 showed 32 percent concordance in identical twins (combining both gay men and lesbian women) and 15 percent concordance among fraternal and non-twin siblings.[4] This is a significant increase compared to a general occurrence rate of about 3 percent in that particular popula-

1. Lisa M. Diamond, "Sexual Identity, Attractions, and Behavior among Young Sexual-Minority Women over a 2-Year Period," *Developmental Psychology* 36, no. 2 (March 2000): 241.
2. Gary J. Gates, "How Many People Are Lesbian, Gay, Bisexual and Transgender?," Williams Institute, University of California, Los Angeles, School of Law (April 2011), https://tinyurl.com/n2gjjgg; Andrew Flores et al., "How Many Adults Identify as Transgender in the United States?," Williams Institute, University of California, Los Angeles, School of Law (June 2016), https://tinyurl.com/hce36md.
3. G. Schwartz et al., "Biodemographic and Physical Correlates of Sexual Orientation in Men," *Archives of Sexual Behavior* 39 (2010): 93–109.
4. K. Kendler et al., "Sexual Orientation in a United States National Sample of Twin and Nontwin Sibling Pairs," *American Journal of Psychiatry* 157, no. 11 (November 2000): 1843–46.

tion. Based on this evidence, researchers concluded that there is genetic influence for homosexual orientation but that other factors also play a role.

A significant paper looking specifically at gene variation between gay and straight men was published in 1993 when techniques were just being developed to survey the genome in very broad ways.[5] Dean Hamer from the National Institutes of Health presented a study that identified a region of the X chromosome that was different in a group of gay men from the same region in their straight brothers. It was a preliminary hint of a possible genetic link to homosexuality. Popular media outlets created controversy by misstating the study's findings, but Hamer's conclusion then, which he continues to state today, was this: there is no "master" gene, no single gene, for homosexuality, but it likely arises from a complex interaction of multiple genes and other, as yet unconfirmed, factors. Follow-up studies soon after in other labs replicated this finding; a third found conflicting results.[6]

Over time, new techniques were developed to look at genes in more detailed ways. Subsequent papers found significant evidence of differences in two primary chromosomal regions, one of which was the same X chromosome region as previously reported, between gay and straight men.[7]

As well, additional research has demonstrated variations, not in the genes themselves, but in "switches" that turn genes on and off in different parts of the body and during different stages of development in gay men. Authors of a 2014 paper conclude, "The preponderance of evidence from sexual orientation research strongly suggests that human sexual orientation has biological underpinnings and that it is tightly regulated at the molecular level . . . we

5. Dean Hamer et al., "A Linkage between DNA Markers on the X Chromosome and Male Sexual Orientation," *Science* 261, no. 5119 (July 1993): 321–27.
6. S. Hu et al., "Linkage between Sexual Orientation and Chromosome Xq28 in Males but Not in Females," *Nature Genetics* 11, no. 3 (November 1995): 248–56; G. Rice et al., "Male Homosexuality: Absence of Linkage to Microsatellite Markers at Xq28," *Science* 284, no. 5414 (April 1999): 665–67.
7. A. R. Sanders et al., "Genome-wide Scan Demonstrates Significant Linkage for Male Sexual Orientation," *Psychological Medicine* 45, no. 7 (May 2015): 1379–88; B. S. Mustanski et al., "A Genome-Side Scan of Male Sexual Orientation," *Human Genetics* 116, no. 4 (March 2005): 272–78.

hypothesize that a network of genes underlies sexual attraction and that this network can predispose for attraction to men, women, or both."[8]

This complex multigene interaction should not come as a surprise. For example, it is estimated that there are sixteen genes involved in determining eye color and 424 in determining height, both fairly straightforward traits.

While the exact mechanism of the genetic effect isn't known, there is a thought that there are genes for attraction to men that are generally activated in women and genes for attraction to women that are generally activated in men that support the survival of our species. In some people, those genes are activated in atypical patterns.

In addition to genetic variation, there are clear examples of physiological variants that lead to gender identity and sexual orientation differences. For example, female fetuses with increased prenatal exposure to androgens are more likely to have gender nonconforming behaviors and same-sex attraction.[9] Mothers of gay men often demonstrate an abnormal pattern of X-chromosome inactivation.[10] Gay men are more likely to be born after older brothers. Each additional older brother increases the odds of a man being gay by 33 percent. It has been proposed that male fetuses provoke a maternal immune reaction that becomes stronger with each successive male fetus. This effect holds even if the younger child is reared apart from his biological family. (This pattern has not been observed in lesbian women.)[11] Brain imaging has shown structural differences between transgender and other individuals.[12]

8. T. C. Ngun and E. Vilain, "The Biological Basis of Human Sexual Orientation: Is There a Role for Epigenetics?," *Advances in Genetics* 86 (2014): 167–84.
9. H. F. Meyer-Bahlburg et al., "Sexual Orientation in Women with Classical or Non-classical Congenital Adrenal Hyperplasia as a Function of Degree of Prenatal Androgen Excess," *Archives of Sexual Behavior* 37, no. 1 (2008): 85–99.
10. S. Bocklandt et al., "Extreme Skewing of X Chromosome Inactivation in Mothers of Homosexual Men," *Human Genetics* 118, no. 6 (2006): 691–94.
11. R. Blanchard and A. F. Bogaert, "Biodemographic Comparisons of Homosexual and Heterosexual Men in the Kinsey Interview Data," *Archives of Sexual Behavior* 25 (1996): 551–79.
12. G. Spizzirri et al., "Grey and White Matter Volumes Either in Treatment-Naïve or Hormone-Treated Transgender Women: A Voxel-Based Morphometry Study," *Scientific Reports* 8 (January 2018): 736.

So, to summarize, while there remain many unanswered questions, genes and other biological processes have a significant influence on the development of minority sexual identities. What do we do with this information? Genes are morally neutral. At the most basic level, genes are simply chemicals that, through a very elegant process, make proteins, and proteins are what direct the formation of our bodies and sustain their many functions over our lifetimes. Genes are neither inherently good nor inherently bad.

Sexuality is biological, psychological, cultural, social, and spiritual. It would be an oversimplification to say that biology is the only factor in its development. But we are called to consider all these things as we enter into relationship with people whose experiences of sexual orientation and gender identity differ from the majority. How will we engage in relationship with people for whom same-sex attraction or differing gender identity is part of their reality—however that reality came to be?

Dr. Mark Yarhouse received his doctorate in clinical psychology from Wheaton College and is currently a professor at a Christian university. As someone who has expertise counseling transgender persons, he suggests there are three general frameworks through which Christians conceptualize gender identity, roles, and relationships.[13]

1. One perspective sees the sacred integrity of maleness or femaleness as foundational and assumes expected roles and relationships are the only ways to function faithfully in light of God's creation.

2. Another point of view is to accept that these gender differences are nonmoral realities, meaning that the person is not morally culpable for their differing reality. They arise because we live in a fallen world, and these realities for some are not the way it's supposed to be, but they just happen—in the same way one might think of a physical or developmental disability. This view generally instills a

13. Mark A. Yarhouse, *Understanding Gender Dysphoria: Navigating Transgender Issues in a Changing Culture* (Downers Grove, IL: InterVarsity, 2015), 46–53.

sense of compassion and empathy in response to a person experiencing same-sex attraction or gender identity differences. But this perspective presumes that something is wrong with the person, and that can be perceived as demeaning or condescending.

3. A third way to think about these gender differences is to see them as part of the diversity of God's creation with persons experiencing them fully acceptable in their identity as part of the community where they can know meaning and purpose.

Any congregation likely represents some mix of these perspectives. As we consider together how to think about these issues, I find it interesting that Dr. Yarhouse proposes that Christians seek to draw on the best of all three points of view: sacredness of creation, compassion, and community. He states, "My concern is that any one of these three frameworks, to the exclusion of the best the others have to offer, will likely be an inadequate response for the Christian community."[14] The first represents a genuine concern from a Christian worldview for the integrity and sacredness of gender and the potential ways in which maleness and femaleness represent something instructive for the church and something for which we should have high regard. The second offers compassion and empathy, realizing that differing gender identity or sexual orientation is not the result of willful disobedience. The third offers the opportunity for the church to provide community and meaning-making to persons in these situations.

14. Yarhouse, *Understanding Gender Dysphoria*, 53.

Appendix F: Adolescent Sexuality

The following chapter was written by Rhonda Walton, MD, who is a member of our congregation and served on our Inclusion and Diversity Study Group. What follows is a slightly edited version of a paper she presented to our church in 2016 during the study process and is published with her permission. Dr. Walton has been a board-certified pediatrician for more than thirty years. She was in private pediatric practice for twenty-one years and then spent a decade serving a charity clinic located in one of the most economically disadvantaged communities of Dallas. There, the majority of her patients were immigrant adolescents. She has served on the Dallas County Medical Society's Access to Care and Vulnerable Populations Committee and Children's Medical Center's Health and Wellness Alliance for Children.

Ideally, adolescence is a time when children separate in a healthy way from their parents and develop autonomy. Becoming aware of and understanding sexual feelings is a normal and important developmental task of adolescence.

Studies show that core attractions, which ultimately lead to adult sexual orientation, emerge between middle childhood and early adolescence.[1] Experience of gender identity occurs much earlier. Feelings of romantic, emotional, and sexual attraction typically emerge prior to any actual sexual experience. Teens can be completely celibate and still be aware of and confused by their emerging sexual feelings.

Sometimes adolescents have same-sex feelings, thoughts, or

---

1. "Answers to Your Questions: For a Better Understanding of Sexual Orientation and Homosexuality," American Psychological Association, 2008, https://tinyurl.com/ybcoysrk; M. G. Spigarelli, "Adolescent Sexual Orientation," *Adolescent Medicine: State of the Art Reviews* 18, no. 3 (2007): 508–18.

experiences that may initially cause significant confusion about their orientation. Typically, that confusion subsides over time, with outcomes that are different for each individual. Up to 26 percent of twelve-year-olds express uncertainty about their sexual orientation, as compared to only 5 percent of seventeen-year-olds.[2] So labeling as "homosexual" an adolescent who may have had same-sex experiences or who expresses confusion about their sexual attractions can be premature and counterproductive.

Sexual orientation, especially in adolescents, is *not* synonymous with sexual activity or behavior. Some adolescents may engage in same-sex behavior but not identify as LGBTQ, because they are uncertain about their feelings or because they fear the stigma associated with a non-heterosexual orientation. Some young people report that they experience same-sex attraction but either remain celibate or engage in heterosexual activity for varying lengths of time, sometimes many years, before engaging in same-sex behavior or disclosing their feelings to their family or friends.

Scientific research has been unable to conclude that sexual orientation is determined by any well-defined genetic, hormonal, social, or cultural determinant, but it is instead a complicated, multifactorial outcome.[3] Many people believe that both "nature and nurture" play a role, but it is important to note that most LGBT individuals report that they have never felt an experience of choice regarding their orientation.

It is also important to note that there is *no* scientific evidence that abnormal or abusive parenting, parental indifference, sexual abuse, or any other specific negative childhood life event leads to same-sex attraction. Nor is there evidence that specific parental actions or characteristics prevent it.

A book published in 1983 by Elizabeth Moberly titled *Homosex-*

2. Barbara L. Frankowski, "Sexual Orientation and Adolescents," *Pediatrics* 113, no. 6 (2004): 1827, DOI: 10.1542/peds.113.6.1827; G. Remafedi et al., "Demography of Sexual Orientation in Adolescents," *Pediatrics* 89 (1992): 714–21.
3. E. C. Perrin, *Sexual Orientation in Child and Adolescent Health Care* (New York: Kluwer Academic/Plenum, 2002); see also American Psychological Association, "Answers to Your Questions"; Frankowski, "Sexual Orientation and Adolescents."

uality: A *New Christian Ethic* espouses the theory that same-sex attraction is rooted in dysfunctional parent-child relationships, specifically a deeply dysfunctional relationship with the same-sex parent.[4] Many organizations that previously advocated for "reparative therapy" relied heavily on Moberly's model to support the idea that sexual orientation can be treated or "repaired."

Currently, all major mental health associations and medical societies, including the American Psychiatric Association and the American Academy of Pediatrics, have published policy statements expressing that they do *not* endorse those therapies that claim to "repair" non-heterosexual orientation. There is no conclusive scientific evidence that this therapy is safe or effective, and it is now generally held that "conversion" or "reparative" therapy may cause significant harm by increasing internalized stigma, frustration, confusion, and depression.

Just *identifying* as an LGBT teenager is *not* considered to be a high-risk behavior in medical and psychiatric literature. However, research has rapidly expanded, and much has been published recently about the effects of reported negative perceptions, parental rejection, and discrimination on sexual-minority teenagers.

There are many studies that report significant health disparities between LGBT teens and their heterosexual counterparts.[5] LGBT teens suffer significantly higher rates of depression and are more than twice as likely to have considered suicide. Suicide is the leading cause of death among LGBTQ youth, who are estimated to account for up to 30 percent of youth suicide annually.[6] Sexual-minority youth experience higher incidents of bullying, harassment, violence, injury, and homicide. Studies also show higher rates of tobacco,

4. Elizabeth Moberly, *Homosexuality: A New Christian Ethic* (Guernsey, Channel Islands: Guernsey Press, 1983).
5. Institute of Medicine, Committee on Lesbian, Gay, Bisexual, and Transgender Health Issues and Research Gaps and Opportunities, *The Health of Lesbian, Gay, Bisexual, and Transgender People: Building a Foundation for Better Understanding* (Washington, DC: National Academies Press, 2011); see also American Psychological Association, "Answers to Your Questions."
6. Spigarelli, "Adolescent Sexual Orientation."

alcohol, and illegal drug abuse among sexual minority youth, along with higher rates of HIV/AIDS, sexually transmitted infections, eating disorders, and homelessness.[7] LGBTQ youth are thought to make up approximately 40 percent of all homeless teens, although they represent only 3 to 5 percent of teens in general.

Interestingly, girls who identify as lesbian have a significantly *higher* rate of pregnancy than their exclusively heterosexual peers, due to higher rates of earlier sexual initiation, a greater number of partners, and less contraceptive use.[8]

However, many sexual-minority youth appear to experience *no* greater level of physical or mental health risks. Increased health risks are actually associated with *reported* experiences of bias, rejection, and discrimination in their environment.[9] Protective factors against depression and suicidal ideation have been shown to include family connectedness, relationships with caring adults, and perception of school safety.[10]

Of note, family-related research has largely been based on reports of LGBTQ youth themselves, and rarely on reports from other family members.[11] As an example, in a study asking youth about substance abuse, they were also asked whether they perceived reactions to their LGBTQ identity from various people (including family, coaches, teachers, and friends) to be accepting, neutral, or rejecting. The number of perceived "rejecting" reactions was found to predict substance abuse.[12]

An additional and more recent risk factor for all adolescents is their growing reliance on the internet as a source of information, support, and social networking. LGBTQ youth who feel disenfran-

7. American Psychological Association, "Answers to Your Questions."
8. Lisa L. Lindley and Katrina M. Walsemann, "Sexual Orientation and Risk of Pregnancy among New York City High-School Students," *American Journal of Public Health* 105, no. 7 (July 1, 2015): 1379–86.
9. Institute of Medicine, *The Health of Lesbian, Gay, Bisexual, and Transgender People.*
10. M. E. Eisenberg and M. D. Resnick, "Suicidality among Gay, Lesbian and Bisexual Youth: The Role of Protective Factors," *Journal of Adolescent Health* 39, no. 5 (2006): 662–68.
11. "Office-Based Care for Lesbian, Gay, Bisexual, Transgender, and Questioning Youth," *Pediatrics* 132, no. 1 (2013): e297–e313.
12. Caitlin Ryan et al., "Family Rejection as a Predictor of Negative Health Outcomes in White and Latino Lesbian, Gay, and Bisexual Young Adults," *Pediatrics* 123, no. 1 (2009).

chised, confused, or ashamed are particularly likely to seek information and support from strangers on the internet if they have no connection to a supportive adult whom they trust. The likelihood of accessing misinformation or, even worse, the possibility of a predatory social connection, is significant. Again, family connectedness and relationships with caring adults seem influential and protective.

There is a common misconception that talking about sexual topics with teens may pique their curiosity or give the impression that sexual behaviors are condoned. However, there are studies that indicate that adolescents whose parents or other respected adults talk openly with them about sex in general are actually more responsible in their sexual behavior.[13] Conversations in this space may be uncomfortable, but they are very important.

Our youth are trying to determine who they are and how to *be* in a complicated world. Adolescents can be described paradoxically as "trying to be unique . . . just like everyone else." The task of guiding them along the journey is an important one for the church, and it needs to be approached with a great deal of openness, prayer, and unconditional love.

How then can we, as the body of Christ, include and support them in a way that tethers them to our community and helps them to develop into healthy, stable adults?

- We can provide a safe place for them to discuss and explore their thoughts and feelings, however diverse.
- We can provide the opportunity for healthy connections with adults who *model* relationship behavior that is affirming, mutual, committed, and empowering, *not* manipulative, oppressive, or exploitive.
- We can, with unconditional love and acceptance, demonstrate that we will walk alongside them through whatever they're experiencing.

---

13. *Talking with Your Teen about Sex,* American Academy of Pediatrics, updated August 8, 2012, Healthychildren.org; J. D. Klein et al., "Evaluation of the Parents as Primary Sexuality Educators Program," *Journal of Adolescent Health* 37, supp. 3 (2005): S94–S99.

- We can nurture the Holy Spirit inside of them, who alone can ultimately change the path they may take.
- We can consistently reaffirm to them that their identity in Christ supersedes any identity they have acquired by human assignment.